UMBRAL POETRY:
MADNESS UNDONE

JACK V. HOLLOWS

Umbral Poetry: Escaping Madness

Copyright © 2024 by Umbral Poetry LLC

All rights reserved.

No part of this book may be reproduced in any form or by any electronic or mechanical means, including information storage and retrieval systems, without written permission from the author, except for the use of brief quotations in a book review.

Any names, characters, places, and incidents are the product of the authors imagination. Any resemblance to persons, living or dead, is entirely coincidental.

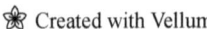 Created with Vellum

__For God.__

CONTENTS

Introduction	xv
MADNESS UNDONE	1
You Make your worth	1
Wordsmith	3
A Letter from God	4
Suicide Note	6
WAR	8
Who are you	10
I don't feel like it	12
What is Love	14
Just a Memory	16
All Grown Up	18
For the Love of God	20
The Love I Never Had	22
Nobody To Somebody	23
Self	27
I'm Tired	31
Homeless	31
Ghosts	32
Second Chances	33
Midnight	34
Grieving	35
The Receipts	36
Who Is The Devil?	37
Remember Them	38
The Thread	39
Depression	40
Happy It Happened	40
Suicide	41
7 deadly Sins?	43
Imposter Syndrome	44
Evils of Success	44
Youth is Blissful	45
RAGE	46

Futility of Mediocrity	47
What They Know	48
Villains	49
Never Forget	49
A Man's Depression	50
It's Sad	51
Time Kills	52
Faith in Evil for Lack of Faith	53
Intellect with Flesh	54
Forsaken Nation	54
Everything is Purpose	55
Escaping The Matrix	56
Happy death-day	57
Living A Lie Is Easy	57
Your Will vs. The World	58
Forgotten	59
Becoming Is Why	60
What About Family?	61
We Can't Go Back	62
Darkness Spreads	62
Love Is Tea	63
The Shadow Within	64
Dark Hero	65
A Duel with the Devil	67
The Pain In Our Hearts	68
I Thought	69
Gave to Much & Carried to Little	69
War Inside My Head	70
How Are You?	71
Alone	72
It's Okay	73
Don't Let Go	73
Thinkers Among Men	74
You vs. Others	75
The Ticking	76
Giving Myself Away	76
I Can't Keep Doing This	77
Drained?	78
Do You Feel Like This?	79
Monster In Me	79
No	81

Devil In Red	82
Forgiven	83
It Isn't Fair To Us	84
Walking Alone with God	85
The Weird Kid	86
Feeling of Growth	87
No More	88
Revenant	89
Chocolate Covered Tears	90
Sacrifices of Good Men	91
Lust	91
The Child Who Wants to Forget	93
Conversation with Death	94
Twin Within	95
Rise	96
Emotions	97
Hi Friend	98
Never-ending Rose	99
Today	100
Love	100
My Darling Angel	101
I'll Never Stop	102
Most ask	103
Me and Me	104
The Crow	105
A Diamond	106
When I say	106
Thoughts	107
Love Rabbits	108
Heaven is Here	109
Spirit Of the Crow	110
The Screen	111
Parenting?	111
Put Down The Guns	112
Life of a New Friend	113
Love You	114
Kindness	115
Young Love in the Sun	115
Is This You?	116
Lion and the Snake	117
Mother's Words	118

If I was God	119
Truth in Chess	120
The Tree Within	120
No More War	121
It's like a Game	122
Energy	122
I'm not Angry	123
This Fire	124
Secret Club	125
Community	125
I See	126
Happy birthday	127
Crow and the pigeons	127
Letting go	128
Love is the answer	129
Cosmic Diamond	129
The Clock	130
Death and Butterflies	130
Expectations	131
Can you see it?	132
To The Next Generation	132
The zebra	133
The Young Elephant	134
Chocolate Heart	135
Do not bend	135
The spill	136
They are also a child	137
I Am Home	137
Mirror of manners	138
I wouldn't	139
We own nothing	139
The Itch	140
The Monsters are Crying	140
All Is Analogy	142
Higher Movie	142
Power is not Addiction	143
Vampire for Wisdom	143
Mom?	144
My Gratitude	145
Righteous Anger	145
Dad?	146

I Never Wanted	147
I Wish I Was Better	148
I CAN'T	149
Have I Gone Mad?	150
Why Me?	151
Why Do You Love Me?	151
Man & Wife	152
That Night	153
No More!!!	154
Get Up	154
Pains Of Progress	155
I'm Not Okay	156
I Went Mad	156
Kids Raising Kids	158
The Walls Come Down	159
"Lost"	160
Here I Am	161
In The Silence	162
Demons In My Head	163
The Games	164
Decaying Heart	165
A Real Man	166
They Brainwashed Us	167
The Two Brothers	167
The Doubts	168
One Day	169
They Don't Want You	170
How God Saved Me	171
Don't Give Up On Me	173
The Vendetta	173
I'd Miss You ;	174
You Don't Want Me	175
Why We're Afraid Of Love	175
HOW LONG!!!	176
No Longer	177
I Was Saved	178
Everyone's a skeleton	179
God First	180
They Would've Broke You	181
Why Suicide?	181
I Still Want To Live	182

What Beautiful Music	183
DO IT	184
A Dream Of Death	185
They Were Fake	186
Why Do We Live	187
A Mother's Love	188
The Love Inside Our Pictures	189
To Be Or Not To Be	189
The Outcasts	191
The Man In The Mirror	191
Together Then	193
The Formula To Life	194
Stop Being A RAT!!!	194
MOVE!!!	196
I'm Not Doing Enough	197
I Wished	198
Mad Poet	198
YOU SAID!!!	200
LAZY FATHER	200
Reality?	202
Devil's Tricks	203
Feel The Whip	204
KILL THE DEMONS	204
Please Father… Forgive Me…	205
The Rose In My Heart	206
Can't Say	207
Ghost Cat	207
"If" I Reach The Gates	208
A Puppet Named Stitch	209
KNOCK, KNOCK	211
GO!	212
The Artist Within	213
I'm Sorry	213
A Day To Remember	214
Letting Myself Go	215
Broken Lover	216
Sad Cat	217
THEY ALL LIE TO ME!!!	218
WORK!!!	218
I Can't Run Away	219
My Cherry Bee	220

This Is Me Taking A Break	221
A Bunny In A Castle	221
The Unreadable Book	222
The Monster Below The Surface	223
The Voices In My Head	224
You Say You're Leaving	225
A Man's Dream	226
Always The Wild One	227
MADNESS	227
Jack In The Box	228
The Demon In Me	229
Why Poetry?	230
They Were Just Meat	231
My Only Wish By: Death	233
I Cried	234
My Love Story	236
Hate	237
Why Not Love?	239
The Hallways Of My Mind	240
I Can Do This	241
This Is Who I Am	242
Who Am I?	243
Reaper Of Rhymes	244
The Ghost Of Poetry	244
I'll Wait For You	245
Deal With The Sandman	246
Wartime	247
Jesus Christ	248
The Lost Sheep	249
Crusader	249
Cerberus	250
PSYCHO	251
Filling A Void	252
The War On Flesh	253
A Lonely Soul	254
A Specter	255
The Pain Of The Past	256
Mandela Effect	257
A Love Not Forgotten	258
You Know	259
A Broken Man	260

The Real You	262
Dark Clouds	263
A Dark Truth	264
The Answer For Life	265
Hey	265
Some Just Hurt	266
Maybe I'm Not The Best	266
Saying Goodbye	267
Why Free Will?	268
Love Is Pain	269
Our Tears	270
Why Do You Hate Yourself?	271
A Walk In Silence	272
I Fell Again	273
Becoming You	274
Let It All Go	274
I ?	275
This World	276
How To See Differently	277
What Is?	278
A Mind Of Broken Glass	279
Bad Dreams	280
A letter To Me	281
DON'T STAY DOWN	282
If I Was Happy?	283
I'm Scared Of Rising	284
It Hurts	285
The Power Of Knowledge	286
Bricks Of Life	286
YOU COULD NEVER !!!	287
Overthinking	288
Self Hatred	289
Chasing Dragons	290
The Boy With No Face	291
Pathetic	292
I'm Right Here	293
Here Am I	295
Horse Among "Horses"	296
The "Hero" And The "Coward"	297
The Dead Man	299
Bad Rabbit	300

www.ingramcontent.com/pod-product-compliance
Lightning Source LLC
LaVergne TN
LVHW030634080426
835508LV00023B/3369

Lord Heal Me	301
The Empty Man	302
The Weight	303
The Eagles	304
Mother?	305
Epilogue	307
Acknowledgments	309

INTRODUCTION

I've been a homeless veteran 4 times, alcoholic, addict, been in situations I shouldn't have been in, have had serious co-dependency issues, and have been a dog for worldly pleasures. I'm no saint, but at one point I thought I was until God shortly afterwards showed me I'm only mortal and why I needed him as a Father over my life. This book is dedicated to Jesus Christ as gratitude for saving me from a life that would've taken my soul, I'm no bible thumper for religion but I am a follower of the gospel because I've realized the importance of the wisdom and way of life Christ calls us to live. It's not just "believe in me or you'll burn", it's following him so we don't fall prey to our flesh and wind up in a hell of our own making. The rest that is in this book is a result of a gift I've been given from God, all glory goes to my Father, I am just a willing vessel with a dream that God brought to life for my obedience. Some of these poems are stories I wrote, and others are structured from life experiences I've lived through, hopefully, by my growth from pain you find pieces of yourself that took me forever to find. I'll be writing from my character's (Jack Valen Hollows) perspective who's lived a similar life to my own, everything here on will be his story and experiences in the world I've created.

If you like the book, please review it on whatever platform you received this piece of art from my heart.

Love y'all

MADNESS UNDONE

YOU MAKE YOUR WORTH

They call you a sin,

To get under the skin,

To break you within,

Don't believe them,

Don't commit self-destruction;

For a half-tailored construction,

Your more than the venom of lowly demons,

Don't wear the clothes they try to force you in.

The best lies have a lining of truth,

Did they inflate your mistake like a balloon?

It was done to them, learned from cretins,

They know not what they do, please,

Forgive them.

Many damaged children walk around in adult skins,

It's not your fault they were broken into little pieces,

Everyday they make fun of others different than them,

Envious of aspects they wish they themselves could fit in.

They pick at differences for lack of uniqueness,

Continue to be a one-of-a-one canvas,

You have harnessed something few get to experience,

A bottomless depth of character riddled with riches.

It's their loss if they can't see the genius,

The light you have will be somebody else's beacon,

Shine bright, never give up the fight, and always do what's right,

Because in the end, that's all that matters,

Right?

WORDSMITH

I come into this forge hammer ready,

I'll beat on words till my bones are buried,

Every swing a testimony to the pain I've carried,

These words are vows to the wisdom I married.

I've been doing this since boyhood,

Spinning golden words into manhood,

Refining my craft throughout fatherhood,

When my web is done I'll be given kinghood.

When I put my soul in the smelter;

I advise you get behind some cover,

The heat itself could be its own wonder,

But nothing compares to what comes after.

Once the world is melted off my spirit

All that remains is an ethereal comet,

This is how I weave speech like a prophet,

I remove pain from love and transmute it.

I fashion a circlet from all my suffrage

Then bring the light of my consciousness,

Setting it in the center as a beautiful signet,

Turning torment into art from my bad choices.

To show we are not our sad past,

That our options are actually vast,

To give faith when you're the outcast,

All is possible if you're willing to craft.

A poet is an alchemist for many a conception,

It's up to them what lens they choose to rend,

For words are great magic you can't imagine,

For this reason, I write to heal the many broken.

For that's the kind of world I want to live in.

A LETTER FROM GOD

I just want you to know,

I washed you white as snow,

I held you when broke,

Always remember: I am always close.

In my eyes you are gold,

In my mind you are the world,

In my heart I created your mold,

In my spirit, is where you find home.

You make me smile,

You may be unbridled,

You may be a little wild,

Yet, you are my child.

Just take it slow,

Just ride the flow,

Just,

Just let go.

I know you,

I carried you,

I am you,

I love you.

Forever held,

Forever one,

Forever loved,

Forever, my little one.

You may run,

You may have "fun",

You may regret what you've done,

But none of that changes my love.

You are my daughter,

You are my son,

I loved you at the bottom,

And I'll love you on the sun.

Here it is,

The key to my heart,

Just promise,

You won't betray me,

My superstar.

SUICIDE NOTE

I found it on the table,

And there I crumbled,

Written on paper so fragile,

It said they were with angels.

I ran to the bedroom

Finding an empty room;

Finding a locked bathroom,

I broke through and saw them blue

Soaking in a bloody pool.

White as snow, ice cold,

Cursing myself a fool

I dialed help as pain took hold.

"Why God" whispering in agony,

My tears fell as an endless stream,

"Why me" squeezing them closely,

Weeping for the ghost of my baby.

I couldn't accept what was happening,

"I know, I'm dreaming" madness circling,

"I'll wake up and you'll be right next me",

A faint hope this wasn't the last memory.

But I didn't wake up,

Still soaked in my child's blood,

You can't imagine the pain that flooded,

At that moment, my heart, gutted.

Please, I hope you understand,

The pain is to much; I can't stand,

This wasn't anything I planned,

But at least now you know -

Why I left this note on our lamp stand.

WAR

You think you're the first one?

To try and lay me in a coffin,

Trust me, I'll paint you crimson,

All I need is a good reason.

Are you going to do it?

Come, walk in the pit,

My hand has a twitch,

My mind has switched.

This is it, got me loading clips,
You chose to be a target
Messing with a marksman,
Your fists won't stop the bullet.

I want peace, you want pieces,
Should've left my kids out of this,
I'll send you to the pits with demons,
I do the same thing to roaches.

This isn't a playground fight,
You flinch, I'll take your life,
Hope you didn't bring a knife,
It's sad if one of us has sights.

I pray to God every night,
Walk away. You still have time,
Or meet this little friend of mine,
He has a funny name, it's "nine".

God wouldn't want this,
Please think about this,
It's your life you'd miss,

All because you thought I'd miss.

I love you, don't let the spirits in

Or I'll have to play the exorcist,

This is a good time to repent,

To hit your knees and ask forgiveness.

But the truth is,

I already chose to forgive,

And the only thing I need to hit;

Is all the parts of you that won't bring your end.

WHO ARE YOU

Shadows of sabotage are grown

From mistakes sown in the soul.

Wearing the old you like a coat;

Sailing away from fear in a boat.

Afraid they might be right

That you can't do anything right,

So you don't even attempt to try,

Letting them puppeteer your life.

Why?

If we were our childish past
We'd still be a child in class,
You did the best with what you had,
Stop beating yourself up to stay sad.

I know that trick,
If somethings wrong;
You don't have to think,
Drinking until you're to sick to think.

Looking to thoughts of suicide
To justify lack of effort inside,
Creating chaos to live in lies,
Instead of change you'd rather die.

I went through this, it wasn't painless,
But I couldn't keep walking aimless,
It was driving me to the brink of madness,
Learning; belief makes you powerful or powerless.

All greats have this in common,

When they choke up on camera,

How they went in to slay the dragon

And emerged with a new aura.

It's all in the mind, not fickle emotion,

Old pain causes you to be conditioned

"Saving" you from stressful situations,

Deep trauma isn't simply rehabilitated.

Start small, be mindful of your thoughts,

Use logic to block mental gunshots,

Recondition your condition for God,

That's how this whole book started off.

It's harder than I'm making it sound

But aren't you tired of being pushed around?

You have the same power to be crowned,

Believe in yourself, that's all you need right now.

I DON'T FEEL LIKE IT

I don't feel like it,

Tomorrow then,

I won't give in,

Just a little rest.

Yet,

Children outside starve regardless,

They don't want an empty stomach,

Nor do they want to be homeless,

Or be depressed with no blankets.

But here we are again, taking time for granted,

We should work on something every moment

Out of responsibility for having the ability,

Others pray for scraps of what we get daily.

Why are we still negotiating?

For a reason to do nothing.

Why are we procrastinating?

On something life changing.

If every second is toward living a dream,

If most minutes spill into problem solving,

If you want it as bad as you want to breathe,

Then it will happen despite your feelings.

I scold myself everyday with this golden rule,

Because to tell you the truth of the matter;

It is true, and that's all that truly matters,

Discipline is the key to the life you're after.

There will be a time for laughter,

But for right now, let's push onward,

They'll whisper your sanity shattered,

But legends don't worry about cowards.

WHAT IS LOVE

What is love?

It is trust,

It doesn't shove,

And it isn't lust.

It's only mission is to give,

Giving way to patience,

Listening with reverence,

Paying attention, without payment.

Love remembers time is limited,

Stopping fights before they happen.

It knows life isn't always fair,

So they hold the other with great care.

If their heartstrings bleed the blues

They'll take them to the moon

And do a little more than spoon,

Making love on their honey-moon.

Weaving souls like tea in water,

Creating a one-of-one flavor

That's made potent as life gets hotter.

You're not lovers, but made for each other.

This is love,

A gift from above,

It only comes once,

So hold onto them as such.

Because they are; the only one.

JUST A MEMORY

There's Someone I used know,

Trapped behind eyes gone cold,

You used to be so full of hope,

Now it seems the world took your soul.

We used to laugh,

Do you remember?

Talking about life;

In late December.

I hoped after all these years

You'd still be a pioneer

For battling your fears; but I find

You're chained to yesteryears.

I have memory of you.

Foggy, yet so clear,

You had a brighter view;

Wiping away others' tears.

Was it the drugs?

Was it the buzz?

Was it the bottles?

That stole who you was?

I need to know why

You dimmed your light,

I miss my friend alright.

Please, wake up, stay alight.

Don't roll over,

We need you soldier.

I know you're tired;

But you're always a fighter.

Show these kids how to live,

Give courage to the hopeless,

Make art from your messes,

Let God give you purpose.

You're my best friend,

Please don't be dead,

If demons are in your head

Roar that you won't bend.

Please don't become a memory,

I want to make more memories,

Be who you told me to be,

Remember what you told me?

You said: "Don't give up, you're still writing your story".

ALL GROWN UP

Swinging in the summer breeze,

Skipping rope in perfect beats,

Running away from baby bees,

Climbing to the tops of oak trees.

Beautiful I still remember these:

Happiness for the simple things,

It sounds silly I know, yet,

I miss the days of tic-tac-toe.

Cotton candy on new year's eve,

The best sweets on Halloween,

Christmas lights that lit up the night

like colorful fireflies burning bright.

When love was simpler,
When it was just love letters,
When a date was playing in the river
And kissing meant forever.

Back when parents were heroes
Thinking they were fighting foes
But were really hiding sorrow
Working until their back broke.

I see the pain they were under
Just to provide for our shelter.
How much my mother suffered
To just put food in the freezer.

So when I reflect on old days
I don't just mourn childish ways
I recall the price that was paid;
And how she paved a way.

Now grown, I want to say,
I will pay her back one day,
I just hope, I won't be too late,

I love you mom, I'm on my way.

FOR THE LOVE OF GOD

What can I say truly?

Other than I am human,

You wrote my story,

Yet, I do not listen.

You cover me in grace,

Still, I spit in your face.

You ask of me so little;

To meet you in the middle.

You say "do right",

The devil in me fights,

Drunk on pride

"I LIKE MY LIFE!!!"

I suffer for my own unruly nature,

Drinking glasses of pleasure,

Instead of listening to my creator,

Discipline, a gift, is made an offer.

I hug sadness to live in madness,

Embracing childish distractions,

Weeping over my poor actions,

Crying for impending consequences.

In life we have two decisions:

To live with light or die in our own prison.

To love as we've been loved

Or sign evil, and commit treason.

Demons bring sweet things;

As offering for the hell they bring,

Angels come bringing a chain;

To pull us from our blissful pain.

We're a slave to one or the other,

We can love God or the devil,

Only one can be your master,

Time to choose, Father, or Liar.

And for the love of God;

Choose your keeper.

THE LOVE I NEVER HAD

To the love I never had;

please don't be sad,

I'll find you one day,

On my life, I charge this task.

Like knights in days of old

I'll face the nights bitter cold.

Rain or snow I will not fold,

Entrust me; with your soul.

Whatever evils come to fight;

Monsters and wolves alike,

Through blood, sweat, and tears,

I will not lose you from my sight.

My eyes may be heavy,

My spirit may be waning,

But I will not lose you,

My sword lay ready.

I'll climb from any pit I fall into,

I'll carry the world if I have too,

I'll move the moon for you,

Believe me, I will see you soon.

Beyond these valleys of bone;

Across deserts of great stone,

Somewhere, you are alone,

I will find you, I will bring you home.

I'll search this earth far and wide,

I'll conquer the stars and tame the sky,

I'll chain the sun and master the light,

All to find your beautiful eyes.

NOBODY TO SOMEBODY

A black heart riddled with scars,

Shame left the deepest marks,

Guilty mud covers their spark,

Branded by regret's watermark.

Empty laughs echo from a soul's burnt coal,

The face says summer but the eyes say snow,

Smiles are rehearsed; just for show.

The stars spoken leak from a heart that's broken,

Saying "I'm not hopeless" for fear of judgment,

not wanting to be seen as someone reckless

"I'm fine, I promise"

yet demons gnaw at them like locusts.

Haunted by memories of old "I can't escape the cold",

carrying loads of stone weeping "I deserve to die alone",

crushing their spirit under the same dark stones.

Disgusted by older images

Resting becomes repulsive.

Voices of love are deemed intrusive,

Anything less than perfect screams

"I'M DEFECTIVE!!!"

Depression is a bloody mountain,

Even with progress; blood still stains their hands,

Even with success; they still see a barren wasteland.

Rainfall turns into death at nightfall,

Each drop falls in harmony to the pouring of alcohol,

Shots become bullets to the soul;

Enticing joy to thoughts of downfall.

Devils whisper memories of yesteryears,

Stringing them to suicide like puppeteers,

Isolated to a cave so lies is all they hear,

Beating on their sanity by shouting

"THE PAST IS HEAR".

Listen well and listen hear, you are not your fears

Are we clear?

The devil interferes because you are a spear,

Afraid of who you'll become if you persevere.

You are not the pages written,

You are the ink in God's pen,

You don't belong in despair's pig-pin,

Working with angels is where you fit in.

Thoughts you feed; bleed onto reflections,

You may have fed the wrong perceptive,

So you can't trust your emotions,

Look to those who rose from darker oceans.

Webs of the past litter the path,

You must burn through them with wrath,

It will be a bloodbath reaching the snowcap,

Prepare for combat, for evil is on the warpath.

Growing colder as you approach your desire;

A monster will emerge from down under

Trying to keep you shattered, pull your sword,

That's all that matters.

This spider is created by past horror,

Pleasure and mistakes are its armor,

The body yearns for its familiar nature,

Fangs coated in bliss tempt surrender.

Ignite your inner fire,

Rage with anger,

Explode with hellfire,

Stand in power, and most of all,

BE A WARRIOR

If it takes you then it takes your family too,

Draining life until you're too weak to break through,

Slowly splitting your mind in two, then no one can save them;

Not even you.

Grieve about what you've done,

But always look for the sun,

Now rise,

For you are the dragon of love.

SELF

Life pulses through trees and stone,

Filled with light from God's throne,

Yet darkness balances harmony's tones,

Everything mended will become broke.

Heat is followed by cold,

The purified invites mold,

To circle one pole entices the other,

Joyful people are haunted by horror.

The harder they fight,
The harder they fall,
No one is immune when the self calls,
A virus waiting for a cut to infect the hole.

It takes one snip to overtake your soul;
But only if you ignore your shadows,
Doing so just builds a denser monstro,
Swallowing your inner child whole.

Making the world no longer magical
Trapped in cynical views you say are logical,
Looking at the world solely as diabolical.
Child-like wonder doesn't make you illogical.

It gives your spirit a beautiful tool,
One you can use to create a world less cruel.
Build creations that inspire the youth,
Rather than painting souls a jaded hue.

Assuming everyone is plotting voodoo causes "lies" in the truth,
Bringing out the worst of those opposite you;

While reinforcing thoughts of "AHA! I GOT YOU!!!"

Paranoid from mental flies buzzing,
Second guessing everyone around you,
Snapping at loved ones from "hoodoo",
Anxiety suddenly becomes instinctual.

Being too analytical can be fatal,
Missing moments that are soulful,
A heartless machine is harmful,
Most notable to your love-starved household.

They don't care about the gold you smith,
Or the "treasures" you buy their love with,
If they're still kids they only have one wish,
To play pretend with your inner kid.

But you smothered your childish self to death,
They try to rise from the dead
Yet you bash them over the head,
Roaring
"STAY IN YOUR DEATHBED!!!"

Was your heart broken so bad you blamed them?
So now there's no more room for them?
Labeling this side within you a problem
You black out this part of your spectrum.

Joy is bound by demons dressed as reason,
Laughing and dancing are seen as weakness,
Life once colorful now colorless,
Colors hiding in childhood images.

A baby inside crying for attention,
Crying for someone to listen,
Only to be met with angry cynicism,
Devils laugh as you abuse them with discipline.

Grabbing a belt you bring hell,
Leaving welts while they cry for help,
Whipping them bare till they're skin is rare,
Lashing yourself for wanting self-care.

Hiding by the slide in the days of roll call,
Hiding in the crunchy leaves of fall,
Hiding in the finger paint on your heart's walls,

Is a little you; just wanting to be called.

I'M TIRED

I'm tired of the old me damaging new things, hard to live in the present when conditioned by painful memories. Getting traction just to lose it from traumatic reactions, I get anxious when people in public do certain actions, sudden sounds fire my nerves like a double action.

Shifting my eyes to find the trouble, stuck in survival thinking I'm still in rubble, spending all my money before it's "stolen by the devil", I get uncomfortable from being comfortable. It's painful to live like you might die tomorrow, no faith in the future so gold gets blown by the morrow, after a while you feel like a sideshow, which turns into motivation to make a better show.

Realizing tomorrow's problems do come I would recommend you invest some then waste the rest on whatever you want. No judgment, I understand stuff helps the stress,

This life is short, so in short, let's grow ourselves to become more than less.

HOMELESS

It wasn't all bad and gloomy weather, at least I found warmth between a wall and a generator, a lot of the others shared their cigarettes too, the smiles and jokes they had lit up the room.

Sure some days were bad but most were good, I got to wake up and go down the street to get some food. It was peaceful to tell you the truth, or maybe that's the lens I chose to look through.

Sometimes there were badmen, and I defended myself like a madman. Which looking back on was kinda funny, I probably looked like a dummy, but I'm happy going "crazy" exposed my "family".

I'm grateful for the dirt I grew from, reaching the top feels better climbing from the bottom, walking homeless in the autumn felt awesome, or again; maybe I just found joy in a bad situation.

Either way, I learned getting back on your feet is all a matter of perceptive, can't really see the stars if you're looking in the wrong direction.

GHOSTS

My past knocks on my door, demons tap under the floor, wrestling myself as I rock back and forth, "I don't want it anymore" whispering in the corner.

Devils dressed as strangers on dance-floors; a carnal frenzy when alcohol pours, treating each other like sexual gore. I covered my eyes from the monster in the mirror, slowly it began taking me over, blinded by the lies my body told. The spirits at play didn't just want parts, they wanted my soul.

Wandering around in a lustful cold, they tried to freeze me in stone, I found my mind sunk below while my body was becoming bones. Drunk on all the pleasures swallowed I became hollow, I woke in the middle of dancing and asked "who do I follow?", looking to the front row I saw the devil.

Suddenly I felt the anvil chained to my ankle, it was all the artificial bliss in which I reveled, trying to pull; though it was too heavy to move, seeing I'd woken they tried drowning me in booze.

"Stay with us, we'll make sure your loved" craving my blood.

Trapped in the same coup, they feared I'd fly toward truth, angels slammed onto the chains that kept me glued, everyone hissed as they rescued me from the devil's room. So even though I'm alone in multiple rooms, at least now I can heal from what I've been through.

SECOND CHANCES

Losing my mind has never felt so good, spreading my soul over pages in a book, taking a second look at all it took to create this book, my heart was broken, stabbed, and cooked.

I wouldn't trade it for anything either, I found the wisdom I sought after, I'm proud I didn't give up like so many others, most will never know what would've happened if they went a little farther.

I searched for a second chance and found it under dark circumstance, call him whatever you want but God does give unrelenting chances.

The love that held me as my mind melted, I felt it, the cards that came up aces, he dealt it, if you have a loving heart regardless of religion then you're a part of his children, seeking the right decisions is the plan to get you to your riches.

Just follow the blueprint to show you deserve the gifts, you'd do the same thing if you were king of all forces, I love you like myself, know you are cherished.

MIDNIGHT

In the mid of night I lie trying not to cry, I miss you lots my cherry pie. You may think not and say it's lies, but you're wrong; for there are tears in my eyes.

These nights are long without you in my arms, misfires in my heart wake me before the alarms.

Sometimes I can barely breathe without you next to me, I wonder through the night where you might be my baby bee.

Yet, beautiful as your memory may be, I still remember how you left me.

I was broken, you showed your allegiance, offenses can be forgiven, especially with penance, but for me that wouldn't break even.

The damage inflicted doesn't have words to fit the description, adding salt to the wound by laughing at my situation.

I have forgiven you, but listen, we're done, over, and finished.

Learning to love myself again took ages, turning to addictions to escape the madness.

Became somebody I wasn't to cope with the anguish, they were my choices and I paid the payments,

But the last thing I want is to be with the one who set the conditions.

GRIEVING

Waking in the midnight hours, I found tears begin to flower, my heart yearns for the warmth of my loving mother, yet only darkness now tucks me in my covers.

Who knew I craved to stay a child forever, such love was found in her arms, I know I won't find a moment better, where I knew the one holding me really cared, she would've laid down her life in the face of any monster without fear.

All for a child who would grow just to feel like a cowardly deer, yet courage outpours when I remember her, in her memory I draw power, it just hurts to know the only family I have right now is the mirror.

No more jokes with brother and sister, no more playing in rivers, no more birthday dinners, just tears falling on old family pictures, I will be a soldier and push forward, but right now I'm coming to terms with being stronger.

So I let my heart grieve for the life I don't have anymore, for tomorrow I continue the path of the warrior.

THE RECEIPTS

Our mind conforms to comments while kids, all the praises hammers in the titles they give, setting a foundation that isn't even you; just concepts others choose.

Wanting to be included we let others pollute our image causing identity dilution, getting older we follow group psychosis into sensual afflictions for social validation. When we wake in the mirror we see the creature we became out of fear.

Being shaped by a world that leaves you as a horrible distortion makes it hard for restoration when you decide to become the solution, now the compounded interest of the actions taken must be paid with inner shame and torment.

Forcing you to look at the old doors you used to open and sit with yourself in judgment, this is needed so you become so disgusted that going back isn't even an option, the addictions then unveil themselves as worms eating your core, digging deeper into your heart while whispering "we are the answer, and your lord".

Something higher than who we are is needed to remove the infection from our tower, inwardly we all know that reason is somewhere within our soul's power.

But if the "why" isn't strong enough, the devil will drag you back with the receipts collected from your old self, so it's up to you what you deem worthy, but personally, running away from the cancer that was me is enough truly.

WHO IS THE DEVIL?

Without what the devil brings could we be happy? Imagine no pain, agony, or misery, sounds heavenly until that's daily, we only crave heaven's gates because we've known suffering.

Tomorrow you wake up and everyones smiling, nothing is wrong and everyone is laughing so hard they're crying, can't feel anything other than the happy feeling.

Is that paradise or forced compliance, is autonomy a gift or a hindrance? Could these emotions and this experience be why we give God so much reverence?

Is this why we receive so much forgiveness because this is the garden of Eden for our soul's to play in? What if we're meant to feel our desires to realize the flesh isn't what we're actually after?

To come back and give testimony that this life is sacred and an honor, to understand every breath granted is only possible through a loving Father, to recognize we owe our life to our soul's keeper.

Only by surrendering to the narrator can we have the nirvana we're after, from us being allowed to live shows the character we're called to mirror. Mercy, forgiveness, selflessness, purity, patience, structure, and power.

This is how we show gratitude for our free will in his world, the devil is just a chisel but your faith marble, each strike is for a purpose but the question is will you hold onto God or crumble?

REMEMBER THEM

God had different plans, but aren't you happy for the time you had? Or would you rather it never happened? Even if it was just for a little bit, wasn't it bliss? Would you trade those memories for anything less?

It was beautiful while it lasted, the moments are still beautiful even if they're in a casket, they wouldn't want your heart to forever have a blown gasket, they'd want you to weave your heart back together into a beautiful basket.

We may never know why you were chosen to hold a pain held by millions, but from your healing you'll save thousands, I hope this is enough to help you cope but I know it won't, I pray you just know they wouldn't want you to stay broke.

They'd want you to find your way back home, you aren't alone in the pain which you're soaked, it brings you closer to others who are on the same boat, and you'll be surprised by how many there will offer you a raincoat.

Which just goes to show how much suffering ties us together like a rope, you may feel like you've been put under the devil's microscope but the truth is you've been asked to see the world through God's kaleidoscope.

To see others trapped in the same foxhole, to help pull them from that hellhole cause they're just you with a different soul, and when your hand takes hold you'll say the same thing you were told

"DON'T LET GO"

THE THREAD

Ripping open my chest to find what's making me feel dead I found a thread, crying from madness I rip at it in hopes of relieving my dread, roars of cynical parents, angry kids, raging men, spiteful women, and shaming preachers unravel in my head.

Pulling harder, out spins a web of images from my subconscious of tormented children. Hitting my knees I keep trying to tear the string from my spirit.

I begin to see more anguish from the sea of my memories, fathers losing wives after having their baby, siblings burying each other to early, sons killing other sons for money, kids turned killer because of an abusive family, little girls becoming twisted from the lust of society, hungry children marketed by companies that barely do anything, addicted parents trying to quit the cause for their child's suffering. As the pain was reeling like an endless movie I began to scream

"WHAT IS THIS!?! THIS FEELING!?!"

Sobbing I begged God to reveal why I was seeing all this agony, then I heard a whisper

"Because your heart is still beating"

Slowly I stopped pulling when I realized the string was my love for humanity, Suddenly, a thought overshadowed:

"They're all just different versions of me".

DEPRESSION

I remember this, pressure I'm a mess gets immense, hating myself for anything less than perfect, what others catch gracefully I miss "unsurprisingly". Escaping into twisted things to numb the feelings of insufficiency, hiding my face to shield others from seeing a disgrace, falling on facts, not excuses for my fall from grace.

Trapped in thought thinking "is this life even worth living at all?" surrounded by copies of celebrities that promote addiction and sexual immorality that find it's easier to be artificially happy than to find meaning. To wake to a world that mocks inner beauty, to be in a reality that shames the holy, to grow in a place seeking to destroy you daily, why would I ever want to keep living?

I found the answer in others that were just like me, we keep going in hopes one day things will get sunny, that's when I learned if I was always happy it wouldn't mean anything, I realized I needed pain to fully enjoy gain, with that in mind I figured out if I stayed the same then nothing would change.

Then lightning hit my brain "this life is a game I can shape if I choose to play", from that day I decided to look at the world I wanted to create instead of looming on mistakes that are meant to help me elevate.

HAPPY IT HAPPENED

Even if we don't feel the same warmth we once shared, I still let tears fall on the memories of the good years, pain may pierce yet I'd rather have some than none moments with you on this sphere.

I'm not bitter, I'm not sweeter, I just understand they can give you better. What you wanted didn't line up with the rest of my chapters, I let you go cause I knew holding on might take you under, the path I wander is one of a warrior.

I gave all over in the hopes another could make me happier, which put unnecessary pressure on your character, I'm sorry I was a lost child looking for a mother, you never deserved the passive aggression I harbored, and I didn't deserve "the lover's lie" when it was my resources you were after.

Yet, I still cry for the shared love as we raised our little girl, I may not be her father but I loved her like my own daughter, when I said

"I love you"

every word came from my heart's fibers. Whenever I look back I don't see a broken family tree, I see an album labeled "a beautiful memory"

I know there were times when you really did love me, and I you, but in the end we were both just love hungry fools.

SUICIDE

When you're a child you find life vibrant with curious eyes, despite the lies there's still a want to find the "why?", as you age like wine your wisdom develops uniquely over time, everyone eventually finds the only thing to do is to work at something until you die.

To make life better by sacrificing traits that no longer help you thrive, but that's when the problems arise, parts that you like must now die to birth a mind that can maintain your desired life.

Easier said than done, actions are seeds planted in the subconscious garden, so when you've spread a seed of pleasurable destruction it becomes madness to cut down the harvest sown to make room for the new crops to grow.

So many good memories are tied to what was grown but they have to go to get where you're trying to go, each swing of the scythe feels like your life up until this point has been a lie, the pain of cutting down what used to get you through the night feels like cuts on your soul-line.

But living a chaotic life for to long crucifies your light to be strong. I should know, I drank so much while playing in snow that I really believed for a moment that life was about escaping the pains of growth, until one day I looked in the mirror and found a ghost.

Hollow from all the pleasure I swallowed I heard a voice echo

"So this is the man you want your son to follow?"

Crumbling to the ground I knew I had to climb my way out somehow, I relapsed so many times while my spouse yelled "kill yourself now!" that I wound up homeless with a gun in my mouth, but in that moment I found the devil went from loud to silent as a mouse.

An angel whispered through my last cry for help "God can heal your broken shell, please come back, so many are praying you get well", tears began to swell as I put the gun down and said:

"God will save me from this hell, the old me is now dead"

---

7 DEADLY SINS?

Many say 7 are the sins, but fail to see without them there's no human, any facet of life that exceeds moderation can become sin, to much of anything is a bad thing including these aspects upon reflection:

Pride is the over-saturation of self-confidence.

Greed is inflated ambition that blurs the line for moral decisions.

Wrath is the sudden eruption of self-righteous aggression.

Envy is the intoxicated version of admiration.

Lust is the result of overstimulated passion.

Gluttony is the werewolf of moderation.

And sloth hides in the shadow of relaxation.

All these facets are needed to provide a fulfilling spectrum for humanity's experience, the real mission is to find a balance in each one to manifest yourself into your desired version.

Create a character equipped for the dark terrain of this creation, pain is a component that's very potent and everyone is looking for the perfect alchemical formulation, but most don't understand the whole point is to make your own concoction.

So just keep making potions until you have a vast collection, when ready, just pour all of it into your cauldron and transmute with final ingredients, just beware of sinful nature trying to spoil your authentic creation.

IMPOSTER SYNDROME

Feel like you didn't earn it? What about all that work you did? Did it just appear out of thin air? Who ran away from your old character? Did others move you or did you push forward? Why are you so hard on yourself? Is it to create a hell to inspire you up the hill? Does it feel good to think you're still ill to ignite your will? Isn't the old you enough to give you the right amount of chills? So why grind your heart with a mental mill to the point you no longer feel a thrill? Is all this torture how you want to live? Do you think the mind would be more efficient if you learned to love yourself?

Of course it would, but will you allow happiness to find you in your dark woods?

EVILS OF SUCCESS

They'll tell you "YOU DID IT!!!" then casually act like they knew you were a walking legend, but before they weren't interested so what shifted?

They see opportunity to use your name to shortcut into fame, it was never about you but the position you gained, once you transcend the tricks of fleshly games nobody has a chance to steal what you create.

That's why they despise you don't drink or take part in the devil's cake, there's nothing to leverage if you live that way, they can't control you and that's what they truly hate, it's time to accept your place.

Walk in the power you earned, speak with authority out of respect for your work, actions are enough to prove you are the king on your board. So no more acting small for the feelings of others, stand firm in knowing you're an overcomer.

You survived the fire intended to break you asunder, so now is the time to bring forth the warrior that kept you from going under, let your presence be lighting and your voice thunder, and if you aren't respected:

Leave the goblins to their murmurs.

YOUTH IS BLISSFUL

Youth is Blissful when raised in a privileged household, no pressure of wolves outside the home, growing older the only thing to do really is just be a "straight A" child and look cute.

Everything will be handed to you which builds a sense entitlement nobody is entitled to. This world is designed to swallow you if you're not careful, just think of human nature, think of prey and predator, think of the conqueror and the conquered, is it a blessing or a curse to be sheltered?

To be raised thinking there aren't any monsters, to be taught to conform to the norms of following orders, you can be rich and still be raised inside a sheep's enclosure, so what happens if caretakers are taken to the grave-digger?

You formally get introduced to the real world, people you've never seen before come to pillage the treasure not guarded anymore, you'll get taken into distant relatives home just for the money that comes

And because you're too young to understand what's going on, they'll blow it all before your grown, by the time you figure out what happened they'll just laugh

"That's the world hon"

But if you were born poor you would've had a chance to see how the anatomy of humanity worked before getting kicked out the door.

RAGE

Anger is how we express our right to live in a world designed to take our life, rage is how we fight when we believe a cause is worth our life.

In this labyrinth of loss you must find a reason worth the cost, everyone has a view of what's worth pushing through the frost, some help the lost, others become a boss, most work then drink until their eyes get crossed.

But if you can find that one cross you really want to carry across life's fog; then you will live in the promise of God, that anything you put hands on you'll be guided to the top.

So what's worth dying for? What's worth crying for? What's worth lighting your fire for? Once you know the answer never let anyone tell you

"Don't bother"

Show up; and show out until you become your own unique master. You're a flavor no one can imitate, a taste so rare that souls get nostalgic when they see the work you display.

So don't be confused or displaced because you belong in this place, and promise me one thing; if anyone tries to take you away promise me you'll

"RAGE!!!"

FUTILITY OF MEDIOCRITY

How much longer? wasting resources to prove to others we're worth it, chasing validation of men and women we deem more than human.

The only difference between us is I believe our hands can be like Midas, I'm the side of you that knows if they can climb then we can fly to the highest.

We don't have to keep wasting our time on flies who only circle around nightlife, they chase a buzz their whole life just to end up with one of their kind.

We only escaped because we're a moth attracted to light, we gravitate toward the question "why?", they may have stunted us for a while only cause the primal mind wanted a tribe, but now you know we're meant to shine not hide.

I've waited for this moment our whole life, to help unify the pages of pain into our story of victory over the night, we belong to starlight, don't you ever forget your side.

We are a holy knights cloaked in light,

we are the war-cry for a higher way of life,

we are the blade that cuts through lies of night,

we are many,

and God is our pride.

WHAT THEY KNOW

So many hide their broken heart-line by acting like Hyde, a cry for attention and validation they never had in life, only a neglectful family that left them out to dry, so when the devil came by and asked "wanna get high?"

How were they to know he was evil when they've never seen the light? Caught up in beautiful lies they were soon adopted and given twisted love instead of having none, so when the only "family" they've known asks for a favor it's already done.

"THEY SHOULD KNOW!!!"

But they don't, only drugs and violent people was their home.

They grew up in a different type of church with roles reversed,

Many had the privilege to travel a path that wasn't cursed,

Many have a family to help their patch their burns,

But these "evil" people only ever had the devils to run to when they were hurt.

Pray for their peace in the midst of the chaos they call home, and don't judge them when it's all they've known.

VILLAINS

Villains are given a bad name, they're only deemed evil by collective judgment anyway, in their minds all is justified because

"Where were you when I cried?"

They developed violence to stop pain from the outside but it altered their insides, who's to say we wouldn't have ended up the same way if we lived their life.

We'd probably be worse, or worser still; dead while alive. Of course the offenses done have to be brought into the sun to be judged, but at least wish grace for a soul who never knew love.

If they did know it and still chose to be the devil's son then punish the demons with the same forgiveness you've been shown, if the actions happen in the moment then do what must done.

But be righteous with the anger that comes, don't become the same monster In the form of a judge, that's what the devil wants, to prove your love for God is limited when set against vengeance you want.

NEVER FORGET

When you get there please don't forget where everyone is at, have understanding not judgments about those who are still trapped, they're still learning the futility of living in pleasurable lack, you wouldn't blame a child for doing bad;

You'd look towards who taught them to act like that, I know you broke your back to unlearn and relearn how to be better than your past, but please show the same empathy God gave you when he rose you from your trash.

There were instances where you knew divine intervention played a hand, the "coincidences" that just happened had to have been angels guiding your steps, so even if you have a Rolex, remember:

Let others see the God in you that brought you through your exodus.

A MAN'S DEPRESSION

In 2022 according to records, 39,000+ men and 10,000+ women are the suicidal numbers on record, almost 300 percent is the difference between men and women, a man is designed to work efficient while a woman is guided to heal the family when deficient.

Warrior and a healer is the union of nature, but life requires much sacrificial labor to get the family security and comfort, the pressure to be better is enough to put anyone under. However, if men don't grow faster then the family suffers, so when a father goes all in for his family's future the worst thing that could happen is when the wife has much unresolved inner torture and forces him to choose between her and treasure, nothing is worse than a woman who needs to be constantly validated to feel worthy of her worth.

For if she thinks she isn't getting enough then thoughts can turn to "I could just take half his stuff", these are just a few fears men have while trying to level up, we better ourselves for those we love while putting our own feelings under the bus, yet if we're not respected or loved the devil begins whispering to us:

"knock yourself off, make THEM carry the cross, only then will they appreciate what you brought"

As men we're not allowed for anything to be wrong or you're considered inferior and not strong, so we slave around the clock to prove we're deserving to be somebody's rock, and even if we do find someone to interlock we'll never be able to shake the thought "they only love us for what we can stock",

but as men this is what we live for:

To move the rocks so our family can walk.

IT'S SAD

It's sad, human nature must war to prove who has the bigger hand.

It's sad, we kill families and then say it was God's hands.

It's sad, soldiers go mad from listening to orders of man.

It's sad, devils in 3-piece suits send the poor man's sons to no-man's-land yet keep theirs on homeland.

It's sad, money can go everywhere else except back to citizens of the land.

It's sad, love has been perverted to treating hearts like used cans.

It's sad, so much food goes to the trash-can instead of pantries for the hungry-man.

It's sad, governments run tests on the people they claim to protect from the bad.

It's sad, pharmacies put price tags on medicines that many need to have.

It's sad, for the lack of programs kids turn to crime to help feed their mom and dad.

But most of all, it's sad that most of us are trapped in cycles of artificial happiness like rats.

TIME KILLS

Time is a slow killer like the falling degrees of winter, at the start its warm so it feels like there's no cause to care, then one day there's a chill in the air, some keep frolicking without any cares while some become scared.

One side keeps acting like there's nothing to fear but the other sees the reaper drawing near, the nights grow colder as the seers work inward to find answers, many slander them for their efforts in effort to merit the life they've harbored.

However, as the snow began to spew they all ran to find the few who left for differing views, finding them at a cave guarded with troops, "PLEASE HELP US!!!" they spewed

"We don't know what to do"

The leader shook his head "we have limited food, we worked while you acted like fools, and we won't pay the price for what your actions brought you"

This is a perfect example of how time if abused can lead to suffering for lack of virtue.

FAITH IN EVIL FOR LACK OF FAITH

In this world of predator and prey it's easy to believe night overtakes the day, most believe this way to justify why their actions aren't toward making a change.

Reinforcing the idea everything will stay the same only cultivates more ground for devils to germinate, every cause has an effect wouldn't you say?

So the thoughts you engage permeate into actions of various shapes, it doesn't happen in a day but slowly chisels you into the shape of what you entertain, so why does mediocrity get glamorized and praised?

To line the pockets of those who want you to resist the pain, they know the brain tries to shield you from growing pains by seeking pleasurable games, so they continuously make "answers" to keep your ambition at bay.

When something is truly painful; people will find a way out to stop feeling that way. So only when being the same becomes more torturous than accepting change that's when a person will change.

For better or for worse, but eventually numbing the pain drives you insane for you know if you keep going this way you'll end up in the grave, this is why some leave the world the next day.

Because it's easier to retreat than to evolve to a better place.

INTELLECT WITH FLESH

Intelligence is by far the greatest gift granted by the highest, when blended with the flesh; however, it can be corrupted, the evolution of our senses hasn't changed but a little bit.

Our concerns are still tilted toward ourselves within, it's an element of us rooted in our blueprint, self-preservation is what makes us human, the wirings of the body motivates actions to take primal action.

This side of the mind pulls your strings while you think it's free will you're choosing, being intelligent means the choices you make are consciously directed at what you want to create; while powering through the reptilian brain when it signals to run away.

Ethical intellect sets the stage to transcend our animal ways, allowing us to forge new ways. So either we can be shaped to the preset model of clay installed in our brains or we can choose to shape ourselves proving that we're the potter of our fate.

FORSAKEN NATION

World war 1 is very puzzling, from one man came generations of pain, Serbia wanted freedom from unjust games the Austro-Hungarian empire played.

As tensions rose from more devilish play; a single man detonated the devil's daisy-chain, the little brothers brought in their big brothers that day, aristocrats on both sides had ulterior agendas to gain.

However, the people were battered by propaganda rain and those who disagreed were taken away, because of few; so many paid. Once the war expired Germany took the brunt of the blame leaving them disadvantaged in every way.

Hate grew from their hearts because nobody likes to be blamed when they didn't even have a say, then along came a man with speech deadlier than a rifle when it takes aim and pointed toward the jews who were doing great despite the starving nation of those dark days.

The hungry and sick clung to hope that maybe this man could really do it, to revive prosperity in the face of a world that rejected them, planting fear while promising answers the country forgotten gave all power to a monster.

All because the world set conditions for evil to prosper in a forsaken country that was just following orders.

EVERYTHING IS PURPOSE

Look around, how do atoms of matter know how to stay fixed to an assigned object? Must be a mind behind the wall, like the wizard of Oz orchestrating the city within the walls.

Seems our reality is made with purpose that takes the form of a vibrating ball, so what's the point to it all? Doesn't the sensations of experience fill you with awe?

The odds of you living your chronicle are astronomical, so much so that how do you not know the magnitude for your potential? Everything here is created and held together with purpose, so you must have something inside you that's cosmic, something only the divine knows when they issued you here like a comic.

Accept your not a mistake destined to work until your back breaks, but one who is meant to carry their own weight to reach heaven's gates, which only happens by unveiling who you are with faith.

ESCAPING THE MATRIX

This is going to be a rough talk but everything is our fault, we're all worthy of choice to make tough calls, "escaping the matrix" is just understanding we're responsible for it all, our pain, our mindset, our beliefs of what we're capable of.

What separates a worker from a noble is the mantle of choices they hold, one chooses to crumble under trouble while the other is ready to rumble. I know it's hard to outgrow a family's cursed outlook from where you're grown, but the truth is; most come from worse and still somehow brought nobility to their home.

How is that possible in the face evil? They made a decision that all actions taken were to be toward escaping the devil's castle, they tore through the lies told to escape a painful cold of being someone else's gold, it hurts to know getting better means letting go of the old.

However, anything that holds you back can no longer be allowed to linger, lest you keep being poisoned by demons who want you in squalor, stand up!

BE A WARRIOR!!!

HAPPY DEATH-DAY

It happened again, did you feel it? Happy death-day!!! I hope today reminds you that all the dramas of day-to-day fade away with you into the grave! So I have to ask: is the gossiping of someone else's ways worth the price you pay?

By the time you finish what you say you've already paid more time toward the afterlife wouldn't you say? Were the words well spent? Did you spend them to build or resent? All that remains after death is the actions you left.

Most don't understand the tongue reveals the heart in your chest while action creates reflections of yourself, so why do others ask for respectful friends when they can't even keep their disrespectful mouth in check?

Why do they ask for a helpful world but haven't helped a soul since eleven years old? Why do they ask for real love when they offer nothing at all except a body with the mind of a doll?

Happy death-day!!!

LIVING A LIE IS EASY

In this world we know one thing for sure: nothing is given it's either taken or earned, if anything is easy then evil is behind it for sure. Think about this in metaphors, moving merch in and outside doors turns into a tedious chore, sitting at a desk shifts into: "I am more", picking up trash alters into a feeling of unfulfilled worth.

Eventually everyone has a choice to stay or fly toward their next course. A nest of comfort vs the unknown world is always scary, especially if you believe the opinions of those you deem more worthy, the thing about belief however is it's just like water, pour it into something you love long enough and you become the model you desire.

Thoughts tip the kettle but action pours the whole pot, people can laugh all they want while sitting on the lawn, one day you'll be laughing about how you became everything while they stayed as nothing at all.

YOUR WILL VS. THE WORLD

There is no motivation when you MUST create your best creation, the choice to cultivate character or be shaped by others is a hard decision, either you're alone with growth or you're around puppets who want control.

Both hurt on a similar level, one brings great suffering as the price for becoming your dream, the other brings great suffering as the price for just dreaming, when you believe it's to hard to be the person of your dreams just ask yourself:

Is there anything else worth pursuing?

Even if your belief doesn't shift for awhile the actions compound into proof you are your acclaimed profile, counter the stacks of old files by filling up a new file and be sure to label it: "God's Child".

A lot can happen when full responsibility is taken, accepting any feedback for future stratagems makes you a threat and asset of boundless proportion, so will you, or will you not, use your will to fend the world off?

FORGOTTEN

We forget no matter how much we wish to direct another's motives that ultimately it's their preference of perspective that's chosen, we forget why we want to live until death almost adds us to his collection.

We forget we like to feel and experience this vexing creation, we came here of our own independence choosing breath over staying breathless, every aspect of life has been done except the moment you were born in.

Every action after is a wonder because how you lived remains unexplored until your exit, we all suffer but it's amazing how others come from worse and still create a dream despite their horror.

Yes, you might be called insane, abnormal, an outsider, or even a monster if you break the norm, but this only happens when a soul truly immerses themself in their adventure, picking up one's oar to explore uncharted waters is what we're here for;

Not to copy someone else's blueprint on how to live a life thats YOURS! It's crazy until it works then they praise the genius in your work. Family, friends, even parents, fade away as you push past the line of what they thought you were able, seeing in you what they buried becomes a sight almost unbearable.

So remember, a 1000 years from now no one's going to remember how you dug deeper, so don't wait to become forgotten by those into whom so much time you've invested just to realize all the time you wasted, do it for you, not for the praises.

BECOMING IS WHY

How wonderful it would be to immediately fit into who we want to be, having learned that our past isn't who we are actually, that it was merely a foreshadowing to the bigger shadow we would be casting.

The longer we live the bigger it gets from the deeds we emit, but the journey is a meter we climb to meet the temperature tied to the degree of character we seek within.

If there were no labor to become our ideal version then fulfillment would just feel like a fabricated perversion, like removing what makes you human in exchange for a preferred automation, that wouldn't be you, just character fabrication.

The reason for life is so YOU can make it, not something given but something earned regardless of the resistance, only then would you feel bottomless joy lying on your deathbed, a feeling of accomplishment very few get to feel in their final moments.

Where you feel the actions you've committed will leave a statement that says:

"A single soul can be significant by being authentic"

But none of these beautiful sentiments could be possible if we could just instantly be the end result of our desired version.

WHAT ABOUT FAMILY?

"I would do anything for my family" is the easiest remark said with undertones of death, but the hardest thing to do is become the one who elevates the family crest.

Someone who loves gives all of oneself to give their best, it's not all about wealth, it's also about spiritual health, guiding them through hell requires your character to be a bottomless well.

This is only possible with an iron will and support from the heavenly guild, the end is worth all the pain you almost drowned in, looking in the mirror at who you became will be the most fulfilling moment.

Knowing you truly payed the penance for the life in which you now live is the ultimate form of fulfillment, you'll know all the tears and stripping of layers were just moments that refined your character.

Old beliefs about yourself won't matter because you'll have new fire from what really mattered: the actions you made when you're life was in a crossfire, from your behavior will birth standards by which the family must honor.

Actions always reveal if someone is sacred or a commoner.

You aren't what you think; you are what you do,

and that's the cold truth.

WE CAN'T GO BACK

We can't keep repeating moments that belong in the past, "devils work hard to keep us in classes we should've passed" but we both know thats a deceitful track we playback to validate going back.

Sometimes we use sadness as a device to print moral permits to justify bad habits, some do this for so long that the brain labels the behavior as "classic", so whenever you make the choice to be epic and the pressure gets immense the mind will send memories of the joyous lies you lived in as persuasion to re-invite the demons again.

The mental chemicals that flip are just the remains of the old you trying to get back in, the flesh believes it knows what's best when growing becomes unpleasant, and if your weak in the spirit you'll spend your whole life wondering what could've been if you stayed disciplined.

The life you want is hard to get for a reason, it turns you into a person who deserves great influence. Not everybody can be royalty, some just want to party and let others have responsibility, but if your willing to pick up the burden most won't carry then you'll be showered with plenty so you can maintain what your carrying, mediocrity isn't tolerated in anything worth having, so it's worth asking the question:

"should I keep indulging in the temporary?"

DARKNESS SPREADS

Where is the line between good and evil? Is it found near

"deviation from the natural?", Or maybe it's closer to "tolerance for the unnatural?"

But the real question is who gets to decree the accepted "normal", we used to watch people kill each other in a colosseum, "holy" authorities used to torture in the name of salvation, some cultures even married off children.

So when did the split happen? Holy vs. Sin has always been the best tool in manipulation's toolkit, the ones who get to say what's accepted are the ones with weapons intending usage if there is no submission.

In human nature "might makes right" is sadly the rule, this also applies to anything that's said masterfully verbal, if an idea is weaved to an audience and pitched in a way that belittles wicked intentions then the line between pure and putrid has practically vanished.

The best way to guard against tactics like this is to instill principles and not morals, to pour ethical concrete instead shifting beliefs about the world.

So where is the line between good and evil?

It's in between a couple of words and your perspective of the devil.

LOVE IS TEA

A woman is a body of water while the man is tea leaves of character, a relationship is the kettle and life the fire, when flames get to hot the women start to boil due to their nature of being a threat detector.

Men in those moments are called to emit the core of their spirit, as the blaze brings forth more fears the water reaches critical temperatures, to which the leaves must continue to pour forth the essence of its flavor.

Some can't withstand the boiling waters which reveals character of soul, and if the flame still holds then the liquid can't help its natural role, so the leaves either have to leave or unfold more flavorful gold.

When I speak of flavor I mean the man's actions and beliefs, but when I speak of boiling I mean a woman's choice to either rise or simmer in degrees.

Sometimes the water boils just right and is filled with the leaves potent qualities while the leaves get feel the warmth for it's being, but sometimes the water boils without heat, and the leaves overproduce flavoring,

which sadly means some just aren't ready to make tea.

THE SHADOW WITHIN

There's two sides to human nature that are encoded into our framework: The Creator and The Creature, one is a warrior that brings order and innovation so we can evolve toward a lucrative culture.

The other is an animal that hungers for carnal desires with the will to crush another if any stand against the outcome desired, denying either builds compounding hatred that bleeds through your noble character.

If everyone piles their duties onto you then one day the lack of boundaries you set will manifest as violence or an atrocity equaling baphomet. Even in nature you can see the heart of the world we live in through the lens of hunter and hunted.

These elements are present for us to choose if we're going to be dissector or dissected, but once you've harnessed this competitive edge others will resent you for having the courage they've suppressed to cultivate the monster within their chest.

But you and me are different, we know if we never embrace our limitations and break them then the only one who'll know of what we were able is the one in the mirror who held back for fear of people.

The goal is once we've unleashed; is to then "get a leash" and direct that energy toward the world we want to see, merging both aspects of humanity allows you to shift perspective toward a desired directive.

You see this in corrupted noblemen how they send the poor's children but not theirs to fulfill ulterior motives, all this to say:

"If you don't have a wolf's intelligence then you won't see the wolves in them, period."

DARK HERO

I wake in trenches covered in guts and blood "why am I always left in the mud?", an answer comes "You always think someone will save you like you would; but they're not you and never was"

My mind wraps itself in madness as I go to war with my morals, I think about my "purpose" and counter it with the one life I get and no more, battling inward for the right course I feel hatred and love taking the floor.

Wrestling for control of my spirit; the powers merge followed by a whisper "live according to the world you want soldier". A fire ignites in my soul "GET UP THEN!!! SHOW THEM ALL!!!"

Crawling from the hole I see a light flickering between two great stones, I begin to stand up but my leg snaps at the bone, grabbing my rifle I belt it to the side and reset the fractured bones.

Standing up again I walk in painful groans, a shadow grabs my ankle causing me to stumble, hitting the ground I pull the trigger to my rifle; turning the shadow's head into vapor.

More start to rise sensing I'm close to the exit, limping closer they sprint to have my light extinguished. I make it to the edge but one tackles me to bring death, choking me almost unconscious I grab my pistol and blew holes in its chest.

Aiming toward the others they kicked it away then started kicking my head, pulling the pin to a grenade on my hip they start to run toward a ditch, throwing it between them I use a corpse to shield me from the fragments.

Covered in bloody darkness barely conscious; I drag myself to the narrow path and a voice echoes:

"only you know about the power you've harnessed"

A DUEL WITH THE DEVIL

As I walked through mist on a cobblestone path I heard steps echo in the fog followed by devilish laughs, walking faster I hear someone approaching through the overcast, I listened for the direction but the sound was all around and closing fast.

Hand on my sword I readied myself for a clash, suddenly I heard "well if it isn't the outcast", spinning back I see a man in black "surely you didn't think I'd let you just leave like that, we didn't even have our final laugh"

As lightning cracked and rain began to fall; I pulled the hammer back on my pistol. "Oh my, it seems you wish to not go back", "I'm never putting back on that mask", he laughs "then I guess I'll have to take you to class"

Pulling the trigger his head tilted as the bullet passed his ear, pulling his sword he came barreling toward, I was able to get my steel out just enough to block his first attempted score.

I ripped my blade toward his vocal chords which he evaded bending backward and kicking my chest like a horse, stumbling back my breath became hoarse.

Laughing maniacally he lunged forward, weaving right I cracked him with my saber's guard, mid-stumble he reached for the revolver near his heart, pulling it midway his fingers were interrupted when my razor hit its mark.

Loss of hand not flinching; he returned the favor by slamming his cutlass into my kidney "that's for all the drinking!" to which I tackled him and landed on top, dropping my rapier I slammed my thumbs into his eye slots.

I whispered "this is for all the tears I dropped", he screamed as I dug for the thoughts on why he thought it was a good idea to keep me under lock.

I no longer heard the rain,

I no longer felt remorse,

Just the bittersweet feeling of tormenting the devil himself.

THE PAIN IN OUR HEARTS

Sometimes my heart cracks a little when I think about other people, I think about their own personal struggle to a level unfathomable, like why did the lady look away when I smiled her way?

Do I look like someone she hates, do I look like the son she lost a year from today, do I look like a friend she lost in a horrible way? I don't assume everyone is thinking foul play.

I think we'll never fully understand what it's like to live somebody else's days, so I pray that the man who said nasty things about me gets grace, because something happened to steer him that way.

Hopefully he didn't lose anybody that shared his face or lose his wife to a terrible mistake, I hope he gets a peaceful life with a second look from a heavenly place.

And you dear reader, I want to thank you for carrying your pain, someone needs you to tell how you not just survived it but live with it everyday, they feel more broken than us and need a guiding ray, so what do you say?

Let's light these shadows up with a smile on our face.

I THOUGHT

When you Fell from the heavenly host, I thought I found a holy ghost, a voice of gold that equaled an angels notes, hearing your story unfold is when my love began to enfold.

When our hands came together my love went deeper; but loving an angel kept me from seeing the reaper, it was a beautiful dream as you danced around my heart with a wire.

I may not have been the best lover but I loved you when your heart was on fire. So when I called from earth to heaven for you to come back when I was broken

- For a moment -

I thought you'd hold me the same way I held you when your heart was burning, instead I heard:

"You're only human"

Wire pulled, watching my heart leave the world I remember the numbness when I said:

"I ... Thought you were different from the rest of the world"

GAVE TO MUCH & CARRIED TO LITTLE

I gave all, to keep all, ignorant, I kept breaking their fall that was intended to help them stand tall, I let my family string me along like a doll because I was afraid to be the structure for which I was called.

When they dropped balls I chained them to my ankle so they didn't cut their ankles, slowly they worked angles, quickly they let me dangle, no more pocket jingle, left me like a fallen idol.

Back on my feet after the fall they expected a feast when I rose from my pitfall

- appalled -

they saw my eyes and a difference under it all, different stature with the mind of a wall, shaking they asked

"Can we eat? You have an overhaul"

The beast responded

"You left if I recall?"

The bond was broken when the ones I loved watched me get mauled, a new one formed to the one in the mirror who stayed with me through it all.

WAR INSIDE MY HEAD

Devils kept trying to turn me back into a broken thing by shouting dark memories to guilt me into relapsing, a war wages inside my head that blazes violently while their drums beat against my sanity.

I ran from them for so long that my heart was bursting, until the one who created me whispered: "no more running", my blood started burning, bones became heavy, the ground began shaking, my heart was racing, I knew it was kill or be killed as my eyes locked with the enemy, I roared

"YOU WANT MY LIFE !?!"

Lightning erupted from my eyes as my hands ignited with fire and ice, wings snapped from my back with scorching light while my spirit was filled with the creator's might; and as the earth began to break centerline I shouted

"THEN YOU CAME FOR A FIGHT!!!"

HOW ARE YOU?

Hey family, thought I'd check up on you and say I love you, thought I'd also say the only way is through, then I thought I'd say you're the only one I know strong enough to breakthrough, but I decided not to tell you things you already knew.

Instead I just wanted to ask to please wrap your arms around yourself so I can hug you through-and-through, you're so very important and unique that I don't want you to feel like you're not already enough as you.

Hope to see you real soon, so we can tell each other all the good news, but for now win those battles, and knowing you, I wouldn't doubt you're close too. Promise me you won't lose hope, without rain there is no rainbow, so once you see it, go to the end get your gold because you deserve it you beautiful soul.

And just in case you didn't get the memo I said "you" 13 times because this whole poem was just for YOU!!!

ALONE

The living room turned into a dead room as thoughts of the past loomed together making a distorted view, sitting in the dark I slowly undid what I used to call truth.

These truths were turning me into a fool, giving away a lot of my tools so others wouldn't drown in their own pool, leaving me to sink in my own whirlpool, I began to see that life has rules, and people I'd help broke them for costumes and jewels.

No calls in my phone I asked

"Who cares about me and my home?"

I learned human nature could care less about my stature, it's only focus is on individual matters, found out my over-giving to others was a punishment I chose to cater, putting parts of me in a position to be broken further.

But I kept giving which tore holes in my heart like paper, at the time I was happy since I believed sharing made us human beings, but the truth is "to create is what we were created to be"

I learned some create happy endings, and some, dead ones, but it's not up to me to pay for anyone's bad actions, I may be alone, but at least I'm no longer paying for someone's afflictions.

Sometimes the best thing is to only give wisdom to encourage others to live with the same independence.

IT'S OKAY

Its okay to feel like it's not okay to make mistakes, that just means you like to grow, it means nothing holds you below, it means you've embraced life's flow, but part of that is accepting no thing is perfectly grown.

Trees don't become a perfect tree, they become one that completes its purpose to be, growing a soul is no different from any other thing, in life you will struggle to thrive but doing so brings more joy to being alive.

Darkness is just the misread brother of light, instead of rejection maybe hold him a little more tight, so you can fully enjoy the lights on high when it's your time. I know it's hard to look at parts of you that you don't like but it's the only way to see you're no longer of the night, dark is just light that lost its spark

- right? -

So if you're not the same person from that broken life then you must be slaying demons with all your might, and even though devils cackle at you through the night, remember the only thing they can do is hide.

DON'T LET GO

The laughter you give, the words of hope you drip, the glasses of souls you fill, why would you ever think you don't fit? Looking outside-in I see a spirit dancing to their own tune and it's truly beautiful to see love move.

People light up when you enter rooms, if a feeling arises that says "it's too late for you" it's only because you're a late bloom and took time for you, there's something inside only yourself can do, can you hear the bells too?

Angels ringing them around because the love you lost was finally found in the same room you left to soon, the one where "work" was fun, the one where hours were minutes and then it was done.

The things you used to love to do never stopped loving you, and now that you're back there's so much to create and nothing to lose, so please don't let go, just be you.

THINKERS AMONG MEN

They say our mind is lost, is it? Or do we just have different thoughts? I've noticed if you don't fit in another's box that to them you must be wrong, and if you don't play along with the accepted delusion then you're socially executed.

They say we're mentally polluted when we're just happy that we refuse to be diluted, they cling to identity labels with pre-made attributes on how to be human; hoping to find themselves in another's notion of wholeness.

To be different is seen as form of madness to be persecuted, parents groom their child's personality while the child is still clueless, not every parent teaches malevolence or instills twisted lessons but it seems being unique is now treated as a mental illness.

Some mothers and fathers think they're saving their kids from persecution instead of teaching them how to be resilient, hidden narcissism cloaked with good intentions, turning their children into the world's image instead of inspiring a moment for self-analysis.

They say we're freaks who're losing it when really we're to observant to the mass psychosis most live in, If a group of rats laugh at you from behind caged glass are you the crazy one for trying to tell them they're in a habitat?

To them, yes, you are, because why are you talking with rats?

YOU VS. OTHERS

So some of you came to tell me what? That I'm a bit off? That you don't like the way I talk or how I draw life with my soul's chalk?

Maybe take notes if you're that bothered and appalled, perhaps the way I dance is what you envy instead of the way you waltz? When did being me become a problem with the mob?

I escaped the lie that I had to be treated like a dog and now everyone still involved wants me to be flogged, all I did was stop using things that kept my mind waterlogged and improve myself with God, all I did was survive an emotional holocaust and learn how to love myself at all costs, all I did was finally choose me instead of what everyone thought and now suddenly there's a problem with the way I call my shots?

This hysteria stems from knowing if they stopped living lies they could do amazing things too, but they'd rather hate others for obeying God than accept the truth.

THE TICKING

I felt it one day, the pendulum ticking my life away, the people I was around didn't seem to feel it the same way, a laugh with a drink to the tick of life's game.

Forgetting we can't get back days, or nights, I used to forget and go out the next night, until I blinked and lived a quarter of my life, I began realizing the poison I drank was fake joy I traded for pieces of my mind.

I began to see how we used each other to justify the loss of our time, becoming aware I became scared, after that I saw scarecrows everywhere, stitched smiles with straw filled characters, I started for the door but felt the pull of wires.

I had spent so long in the underworld that I was becoming tethered, as I got closer to the border hands started to caress and voices whisper:

"We want you, forever" as they clawed at my chest.

AS each step got heavier I suddenly collapsed at the doors; and as the devils came to collect their shares my Father threw me over his shoulders and said:

"This one isn't yours."

GIVING MYSELF AWAY

I remember giving away my will and joy to others who treated me like a toy, memory stained feelings of an abandoned boy who gave away all his toys to fill a void.

I let them have everything to drown out the voices telling me I was a broken boy, their happy noises filled me in a way materials couldn't hope, but my soul was dulled by using others joy to feel whole.

A beautiful delusion until poverty broke the illusion and made oh so clear their intentions, that my generosity was seen as naivety to be drained completely.

Then when I needed saving it wasn't the ones I helped that came but a stranger who gave me clarity while I was still in the grave, looking into the deepest part of my heart-line they vied:

"I think its time to start building your own life."

I CAN'T KEEP DOING THIS

Being with a soul that's also broke pulls us both from becoming whole, I can't keep putting myself through hell, I can't keep pretending everything is well when I fall for love spells.

It's at a point where I know the depth of this well and to willingly fall in is an insult to the angels who warned me before I delved, how many times does my heart have to die until I stop living a revolting lie.

Knowing the truth means no more grace for lies, that's why others hide when you show the light, ignorance is understandable but choices between good and evil determines your side.

It's not beyond God to let you walk in the dark with protection so you think it's fine but only to see how far you'll cross the line, to see if you'll do what's right or dance with the devil all night.

I felt the anvil, the weight of guilt, by choosing what made me ill then asking God to heal; who was the one getting the bad end of the deal? How could anyone claim love for someone then sleep with eels? I found out that's how God feels when we choose the world over his plan...

And that's real.

DRAINED?

I stopped spending so much money on abusing my senses, maybe that's why I was so depressed, draining the chemicals in my brain for happiness to then end up feeling hopeless.

I guess hormones and diets actually can make your soul feel rested or lifeless, looks like teachers of spirit were right about fasting and abstinence, allow the mind to reset after straining it with pleasure pits.

It's good for the mind to rest in order to bring back a positive mindset, the ones who are obsessed are the ones most people seem the most impressed, but monks find fulfillment in stillness instead of puffing their chest, I've learned it's really a matter of perspective and honoring a different lens.

Let the beasts compete, let the sheep eat, let the eagles live free, and while we're at it, let God judge the enemy.

DO YOU FEEL LIKE THIS?

I'm so tired of empty talks, pretending to like me and all, what could it be? The sunshine in my walk, the moonlight when I talk, the bottomless depth of my thoughts?

People seem like stars that are far-off from the world I'm on, everyone has their own suite in the cards but when I try to fit in the whole deck blows apart.

Wildcards don't even know the face of my card, the only place I fit is the dark, only there can the enigma of my soul ponder far, the quality of my mind isn't gold, it's a blackhole of wonders untold.

I dream so much the sandman says "welcome home", I think so much the universe is in my bones, I'm so alone that me and death talk on the phone. Being a shadow isn't hard

Just look how others hurt each other for power to control another's heart, then you'll understand why it's better to put time into mastering your own art.

And why you should be in the shadows rather than a world that tries to tear you apart.

MONSTER IN ME

From the grave of a brainwashed psychosis I start to become conscious when I hear a child scream in my unconscious, stopping my walk I looked up and saw monsters herding the lost.

Suddenly pushed from behind by a man who had empty stare

with a locked jaw I look ahead to see everyone going toward a factory labeled:

"The Ball"

Looking closer I see demons putting pins in people's heads like voodoo dolls, inside I see them dancing to music enticing them to have sex in the halls with horned guards mandating everyone has to be drunk to be in there at all.

The owner came on the intercom

"YOU COULD DIE TOMORROW!!! DO WHATEVER YOU WANT!!!"

They began to grope each other near the front, the devils were harvesting souls by urging our primal nature to ungodly affronts, the child inside cried "what about us and our wants, is this what we really want?"

Almost crossing over my anger erupted "NO!!!", seeing I woke; devils jump down to drag me into the hole, as they get close my blood went cold, shadows took hold forming a dark armor of skull and bones, slamming my hands together I state: "We're going home"

Pulling them apart, swords of shadow and bone emerge from my palms, the demons shook "Re- remain calm..."

calmly I reply:

"I'm going to destroy you all."

NO

"Hey... You Okay?"

I get it now

"You get what?"

I get why most stay in what they know

"Why?"

Learning makes you feel like a 8 year old

"Let's just go back then, to be honest this changing thing is getting old"

I don't want to go back to being broke

"Admitting this level of change is to much for you doesn't make you a useless bloke"

You know why I won't go back

"Becaaause feeling good just blows?"

To be who I was would kill my soul

"Oooohhhh, here we go, let the drama unfold"

You were just as disgusted with the way we sold our value for fake emotional gold

"I rather enjoyed it though, having a drink while people cheered made us feel like a exotic islander, you're the one acting weird"

That's the problem with you, you're only good for carnal desires.

"I mean... what else is there?"

Building humanity higher, pursuing purposeful matters, fulfillment of our soul's desire

"But that means we have to work harder, why sacrifice all this pleasure for something we might never acquire?"

I'd rather live in great character than promote addiction and mediocre banter.

"Woooah, so high a mighty all of the sudden aren't we Mr. Liar?"

Not this time

"Not this time what? You know how this goes, you try and change then relapse into being the same with emotional overtones."

This isn't a game, you'll fade one day all on your own, I understand you're the ghost of the actions I've sown, but this time I'm going to reach home

"YOU'LL NEVER CHANGE!!! JUST GIVE UP HOPE!!!"

- No -

DEVIL IN RED

I met a someone who said they'd love me like a rose and before I knew it I was grabbing together all my clothes and going to a place that felt like Rome, across the air we arrived at "home".

I went to carnivals and fairs, shopping clothes of every layer without any cares but eventually something felt weird, like they didn't actually care.

It soon became clear my body was all they cared, not my character or heartfelt layers, I had a breakdown of an ungodly scale, breaking in ways only the divine could repair.

I left all of the treasures without a second stare because in the end I only came for a love that wasn't even there, that's when I truly surrendered the rest of my life over.

That pain, that chapter, that darkness, could no longer be allowed to damage me any further, I had fallen to the level of an animal and needed some Godly figure.

Only something of a heavenly nature could help me get better, so when I say Christ saved me from that fire I mean that with every fiber.

I was a liar, an adulterer, a betrayer, a sinful coward, yet he called me a like a broken little brother, and after all he's done for me I would rather die then go back to being a world worshipper.

I Love you Father.

FORGIVEN

Deep in thought I had a serious talk with God, I asked "could anyone be forgiven for what they've done?".

God said: "aren't they all my children?", "but God what if they were evil and were just trying to get into heaven?".

God said: "isn't that what you and others did?", "God, surely what I've done isn't as bad as them?".

God said: "who gave you permission to do the measurements?", "then Father how do you forgive?".

God said: "by the pain felt in their hearts for what they did and begin to live how I want them to live, remember how you did this?", "but God aren't certain things too horrendous?".

God said: "You think if you went through the same experience you'd come out different? With the exact mind, traumas, and horrors they witnessed? I could put you there if you wish to prove this?", "God it isn't fair to the innocent ones who were taken advantage of, or the ones killed because of their sins".

And finally God said: "who said they killed anyone? It's not beyond me to move a soul from one life to another to let loved ones learn lessons. My children that were taken advantage of will save others from themselves when they heal their essence, you say it's unfair, I say it's the price of free will. Many monsters wouldn't become monsters if many didn't help create their conditions, there was no program, there was no one reaching out, there was nowhere for them to go in the town. So their sickness left untreated was cultivated in that same darkness you and others choose to forget...

And they say I'm careless."

IT ISN'T FAIR TO US

The first time we broke up, broke us... Each time we come back to mend whats broken our standards to be together get lower, then we hurt one another by pretending the other is the person that damaged us before we partnered.

I see the degree of dysfunction clearer than the old me and it's not fair to be so emotionally weak that we keep thinking its a good idea for fire to be with a tree, I can't keep stripping my heart so your ego has something to eat and I can't keep using you to validate why it's okay to be me, we were both to broken to leave, so angels showed me who'd you be if I seemed "Crazy".

I was left out on the street with nothing but the shoes on my feet, you weaponized time with my child as a tool for controlling me, told me to kill myself when my soul could barely breathe, tried to get me locked up institutionally by saying I was deranged mentally, then you ask to get back together when you see me doing better without you evidently...

No...

This time I'm being the change my family has never seen, and the same God you had a problem with is going to turn me into royalty.

WALKING ALONE WITH GOD

The narrow path I walk is filled with grass lusciously soft, a road paved with roses with beautiful birds aloft, angels guard against creatures that have malevolent thoughts.

When I look far-off I see my destined spot yet I hear joyful people below the rocks "Hey, come take a shot!", at the edge of the grassy top "maybe one or two" I thought.

A hand landed on my shoulder as I almost stepped off

"So the promise you made didn't matter after all"

Hitting my knees I remember what happens if I fall, that I insult the very being who saved me from falling walls, the one who was with me through every fall, who always answered my call, but worser still; I prove I wasn't who I said I was at all.

Feeling the dead weight of who I was begin to shed I feel the twin trying to get back inside my head "it's only one more time surely he'll understand, people there need your charming wit to help repair their mental threads"

God grabs it with vicious intent "you won't keep taking my child back to the depths", crushing the devil between his fingertips, he picks me up and whispers "Rest", carrying me while he heals the heart in my chest I look up at him and say:

"Father, you're the best".

THE WEIRD KID

Sitting at my desk I wondered why others wouldn't look me in the eyes, it was like an unspoken rule to not talk to the "freak who laughed at life"

I made jokes of every type just so I'd be liked, I learned people loved to feel alright so I became a clown of light, causing bullies to target me most of my life.

Sensing I was weak inside they tried to kick the joy out from behind my eyes which caused thoughts of suicide because at the time I thought

"why else would they try to stomp out my lights other than I have an unnatural mind?"

Hating myself I tried to fit into all different kinds of lives which only felt like lies, so then I got involved in alcohol and the ways of night, feeling alive I fell deeper into the devil for a time.

Actions which for the most part felt fine until I started to hurt friends chasing lustful and prideful highs, eventually leaving the childish ways behind I decided to join the army because I believed I wasn't that bright.

But that choice still forever changed my life, they helped me become more accountable and organized by the time it was the end of line which gave me an outlook with new eyes, so it turned out I was only miserable because I had no father to provide me with a resilient ordered mind,

Weird right?

FEELING OF GROWTH

I feel it coming... I don't understand why these tears are on my cheeks, I was fine a second ago then my face started to leak, what could it be? Is it the years of being nobody's favorite? Maybe it's fear that the layers I've created are just persona fabrication? Do I feel my personality is just defense mechanisms?

Do I only like the things I like because others don't which gives me a sense of autonomy I chose? Am I pretending to be something I'm not so others will notice what I pretend to be? Is it the pain from thinking if I had a functional family I would probably enjoy life like other happy families?

Maybe it's the wisdom I shouldn't have a partner until I can also lead so I'm not just useless meat? Could it be I'm mad at myself for all the times I naively believed someone when they said they loved me? Or is it how I try to mash together incomplete beliefs so I feel like I can finally stop trying to feel complete?

Honestly, I think it's just the understanding I'm becoming something I can't fully see, I guess this is how the greats felt before they felt free.

NO MORE

I didn't care if they thought I should've never been born, if I never took a stand I would've been swallowed by the underworld, even in nature the weak are eaten by carnivores, it's just the natural order.

I thought "if others can take a piece of the world then for DAMN SURE I CAN BE MORE!!!", they picked at me while little so I wouldn't grow my power but tables turned when I got my own corner.

As I got older I saw they drank away their strength,

I saw they smoked away any stamina in their tank,

I saw they drugged their mind blank,

All of them fell down the ranks.

By the time they realized I got bigger they saw my size and realized I had them cornered, emerging from the shadows they saw my face had become that of a spider.

They screamed in terror as my smile got wider, looking around they saw webs blocking every door, they fell to the ground as I shrieked with laughter, smelling fear, new-found instincts roared "DEVOUR", they screamed in horror "WHAT ARE YOU!?!",

I whisper:

"A Monster"

REVENANT

I was casted into a hole with death, but no one expected us to become friends, as we talked I started to only listen, his sentences sounded encrypted, reflecting on them I eventually broke the encryption, when he saw I knew the secret, he said:

> *"remember, emotions are distractions to keep you thinking you have a limit, that's why they keep distracting you, so you don't become limitless."*

I look up with a smile "I think I've been in this crypt to long, don't you?", he laughed "break your limits then, won't you?", slowly approaching the wall I released all the rage in my soul,

An element of my nature I never let take hold, shadows began to unfold infusing dark powers into my bones and as my heart ran cold death roared "FORWARD!!!",

Running up the walls on all fours I developed a taste for far more than what I used to ask for, the closer I got to the top I felt a shift in my core

And as my hands slammed over onto the ground floor while pulling myself out of the underworld rain began to pour, but when I looked into the water I realized I didn't look like me anymore

Death said: "what do you think of being reforged?", turning towards I say

"like looking in a mirror forevermore."

CHOCOLATE COVERED TEARS

When you quit addiction's medication you find out how much you used it to escape the heaviness of feeling inadequate, you see just how much that hole was filled by that thing poisoning your spirit, you feel like you can't live without it when your demons begin whispering again.

The problem is the devils were always there, they were just drowned by the numbness we hid them under, but as we become sober they still have something for us to think over, I understand the pain of knowing you have to change in order for things to change for the better, but we both know it's easier to live in cycles of the substance abuser than change our behavior.

Yet the sickness will still condition our health for illness and chip away our years regardless, the moment may feel like heaven but the actions you sow could be visually reaped by children, even if you say "don't follow in" your actions says different, I hope you choose chocolate covered in tears rather than dementia-ridden psychosis, sure it still feels fun but only because we haven't tried to live a life where we become someone who isn't addicted to drugs long enough.

SACRIFICES OF GOOD MEN

As I sit in my chair and let my mind ponder, I couldn't help but wonder about men and the role their under, we all know that man was built stronger with a strong temper, so it only makes sense they would do all the work and let the mother nurture.

But then I thought about the pressure of being forced to be smarter in order to provide better, as humans we all want to feel pleasure but the most accessible kind only brings the mind down further which means the ability to do better gets lowered which causes our family to suffer, growing starts to feel unbearable as we eventually think we're only a tool to be used until we aren't useful any longer, thoughts about our wife leaving us for another she predetermined becomes more real the longer we look at the numbers.

Yet, good men hold onto the knowledge that without them the family would crumble, so they make those sacrifices look simple because a good man knows its not about him any longer, it's about the principle of being a great father, he sets the example for his children on how to live in a world going under, he knows chaos may invade his family's borders if his guard lowers, he sets the bar high to make sure his family stays ordered, but most of all he knew when he said he loved his family that he was going to war with his monsters.

LUST

"Hey, how are you baby?"

Get away from me.

"But why? Don't you love my feeling?"

Every-time we get done dancing my strength is left sickly.

"Duh, we always rock the bed baby"

Stop pretending to be something you're not demon.

"aaawww, my heart, how could you say such hurtful things?"

Because of you I can barely look at people without thinking perverse things, it's almost involuntary.

"Not my fault you can't resist abusing your natural morphine to twisted movie's sweetie".

Exactly why you need to leave.

"No, I rather enjoy tempting you to your baser instincts, I love how you eventually surrender like a doggie in heat".

You only want my will drained so I don't complete what I'm making, you know my creation will damage the devil's body.

laughs "So cute when you're all dramatic, trust me, nobody's worried about an anxious addict".

Why are you here then? Trying to twist my actions?

"I believe you should also feel some pleasurable senses".

Earlier you enjoyed my torment, now you say you want me to feel happiness? You sound like a soft-headed temptress.

"YOU WILL BEG ME TO SUCK THAT ENERGY WHEN IT REACHES FULLNESS"

laughs What happened to that ironclad confidence?

THE CHILD WHO WANTS TO FORGET

Sitting inside my head I hear a child cry, I look through all the corridors, but I can't seem to find the child that cries, from the backdoor of my mind he finally came toward, I dry his eyes "why do you cry little warrior?"

"I- I- want to forget and not remember anymore", I see he's gasping more and more "what bothers you, I'll make a cure", shaking he replies "the memories making our heartsore"

Choking, I murmur "we can't... I've already tried", he tears up more "what about the juice we used to pour?", my voice gets light "I'm sorry I buried painful sights by getting us high, but we can't keep letting our mind die so we can hide."

His knees hit the floor "but I can't take the voices no more! They roar our choices and words could've been more! They keep opening and slamming doors! They keep pounding against the floorboards!"

I pull him close "We have to be brave, alright? To get our dream life we have to reflect on what they say for a time, we'll turn the bad input into good output to better thrive", he whispers with broken words

"Will you hold me then? At least until we win the war?"

Tears falling I say:

"Of course"

CONVERSATION WITH DEATH

"Why do you keep thinking about me?".

How can I not? What's the point in living if the end is just to rot.

"Ah, you're trapped deep in thought".

Yes, and honestly I'm starting to think pleasure is the point of it all.

"You only got half the ball, but still pretty good for a life so small".

Tell me the other half then please, I'm beginning to lose sleep.

"Well, perspectively, it depends on what you want to see subjectively, you could choose to look at the whole of humanity and see how they're always advancing, or you could look at yourself and keep chasing ideas you think are fulfilling. Ultimately it's your life so spend it in a way that seems worth investing, but I've noticed whatever you pick you'll still be used to fulfill a plan beyond comprehending".

What do you mean? What's the grand scheme?

"I know you see how people work together to complete different functions like a machine, some want to be seen, some just want to see, some want to clean, some to be a part in another's dreams, some want to drink while getting lost in an artist's fantasy, whatever you choose you'll somehow play a part in destiny".

So what if I just want to have sex and drink?

"Then you become a link in that chain but still do some kind of work to pay, so you'll work a job you probably hate in order to help finance a world another creates, you want worlds of sex and drinking games? How hard you work determines the levels in which you get to participate".

So you're telling me this is all about what life I want to create?

"Yes, and whatever action you take still creates something, so even if you do nothing, that's still an act of creating".

You never answered my first question, why do we rot after learning so many lessons?

"Would life be as fruitful without conclusion? Life's beauty isn't found in an immortal dimension, but found in the struggling for wholeness despite the ticking resistance"

TWIN WITHIN

Walking into a boundless room I see only a rounded table, there seems to be a border across the center where light has an inverted spectrum.

As I approach I begin to see someone else in the distance, they mirror all my movements to which I become suspicious, the closer I get to the table I can somewhat start to see their presence.

Only a yard away I see it's a variant of me with a different composition, we both take a seat across from each other divided by a spectral canvas.

"So who are you" I ask perplexed, opposite me the man tilted his head as if curious "I'm the side of you that refuses to submit", my eyes widen as I grasp the situation "so you're the reason for all our impulsive madness"

He laughs with his hands drumming, then suddenly stops silently "I'm the only reason we seem to have fun any, you keep enacting so many rules that we're barely living", slowly I lean in with my hands cinched

"You only think that poisonous life is the way to live because it's the old blueprint I used implement", rage seething through his teeth with a clenched fist

"YOU MEAN ME!!! I IMPLEMENTED! It felt amazing, still, you want to wash it all away like it never happened!"

I stand up with a look of disappointment "it did happen, which is why I no longer want any part of it", as I walk away he begins to roar and slam his chair on the table's board

"I WON'T BE IGNORED, I'LL FIND A WAY OUT OF THIS MORGUE, I'VE ALREADY TAKEN CONTROL OF YOU ONCE BEFORE!!!"

looking back before I close the door I say:

"I'm not an animal anymore, good luck getting past my sword"

RISE

"What's the price to own the sky?" asked a pair of young eye's, "sacrifice" said the guide, fright burned bright in his mind as the elder smiled wide "anything worth having always comes with a fight"

His words carried shivering truth like chilled light "this price of sacrifice is paid to father time so you may earn the right to be worthy of your desired prize", "but how will I know when the time is right?"

To which the elder replied "When you feel alive... When the fire in your stomach can no longer be contained inside, you feel not a want but a need for what you seek, this is how you will know it's worth your energy, so when you find that feeling remember its an insult to bring anything less than your inner beast"

The child began to tremble "do I have to be a monster just own a piece?", the wise man laughed almost to a wheeze "there are many who compete for the sky, to the north, south, west, and east.

They don't just want pieces, they want it complete and are willing to fill the resolve of character you won't bring to compete". The boy becomes angry "why does everyone have to be so mean, why not share with everybody?", to which the elder whispered

"Because it wouldn't be fair if everyone was the owner of someone's dream"

EMOTIONS

Be careful with emotions, they will chemically control your motives if you have the wrong memories tied to emotional notions of what love is. It's not all roses but it's closest when you're whole within.

Wholly understand you are a holy being When you choose that state of being, no more identifying with an identity we left behind intentionally, anyone should be redeemed if they truly seek forgiveness and peace, at least, that's what I was told by G.O.D.

Let's give our best as gratitude for our breath, no more negatives in our heads, positives explode in our chest when we rise to the test; but I attest I used to detest thoughts of becoming intelligent, but when I surrendered to the heavenly intelligence I became a lyrical genius of alchemical proportions.

I figured out our illustration of life isn't perfect because we run from God's narration, who better knows our gifts than the one by whom we were created? God is not a religion, there is no "right way" to provide worship, but this sentence is the very essence of how God wants us to live, it says: "love others as I have loved you" and the fact we have breath is enough to say:

"I want to do this"

HI FRIEND

Hi friend, did all that fire fry some wires? Lashing out because you just want to be admired when you're already an unfolding work of art to admire.

Underrated on everyone's charts while love chases your heart, pushing it away with both arms, searching for it in someone else's many hearts when they might also be in the dark.

The love you give also belongs in your own heart. I know you're aware if nothing is wrong then there's no reason not to grow, many break themselves further to avoid letting go of the life they've known.

To try and stay in a shell you've outgrown will just crush your soul. Closing your eyes to answers you've reaped from actions sown only causes pain that cuts deep into your bone.

Screaming

"I SHOULD'VE KNOWN!!!"

But you did know, the silence just got to loud from being alone so you left your wisdom for a false hope, every-time you leave yourself there's a piece of divinity in you that cannot cope, and will punish the psyche for abandoning the mission to become whole.

You will always be dealt cards that seem unfair or cold but there's no telling what could happen so please don't fold, even if you bluff,

look bold,

life will forfeit the gold not because of the hand you hold, but for the fire in your soul's bones.

NEVER-ENDING ROSE

Was it you or I all those years ago, where we just flowed together down this road, as we begin to let go we look at each other and know that we were always gold.

You and me will never grow old for we are the never-ending rose, forever connected to those that will always help us flow. In this connection we eternally know that growing is the only way to go.

I love you reflection of my soul, everyday we break ground

for the building of our home, can you feel it? We're so close, don't give up hope, push the plow through the snow.

Actions of growth are loud, we see the end and hold our head up proud, we are a beacon for souls who escaped the devil's breeding grounds,

We are the warriors in the front when the horn sounds, we are the ones who don't beat our chests but pound, we are one of many who serve one crown

And if you're reading this then count yourself among the proud, and God told me to tell you to keep up the fight because you're one of the strongest angels around.

TODAY

Today is okay to say that you're not okay, today is where you lay your head down and pray, today it's okay to let your heart sway and feel all the feelings you hid-away the last couple of days, today is where we both say "tomorrow will be the brightest day" while we kick up our feet and laugh away the yesterdays, have a blessed day and slow down the pace because life isn't about finishing the race but evolving everyday and praying you come in last place, Enjoy your Grace.

LOVE

An energy that's been here since the beginning, mothers and fathers hear the drum beating, brothers and sisters this gives us meaning, belief there's hope for every heart beating to change from pain to believing.

Remember the pieces when you fell down defeated, remember wishing someone would encourage you to keep living? Tell me, how did you rise to your feet then?

Validation from others didn't keep you breathing, especially after all the shame, humiliation, and bullying, yet you managed to keep laughing while making it happen despite what happened.

Astonishing, thank you for being divinely present to save others with your presence, you are a fundamental essence, if your light was ever absent angels would cry because we all need your radiance.

You are not pages written but writing, so keep fighting, for you are the lightning in the clouds most frightening, you even have God smiling, love you family.

MY DARLING ANGEL

My darling angel from every angle, my heart does a jingle when you comb your fingers through my heart's tendrils, every time you giggle my toes wiggle and I can't help but give yours a nibble.

When I saw you on the court of love I double dribbled, can't help I'm a love rabbit and your words are my favorite kibble, you're the realist love thats 3-dimensional.

Wrapping you in the folds of my soul I'm careful because I know you're a damaged angel, I love you my sweet cherry petal, we'll age like wine and weave our soul's into a golden metal.

There's nothing I wouldn't go through if it meant seeing a smile from you, truly you hold my sanity like glue, truly you shade my soul a brighter hue, truly you heal my heart in a way only you can do.

But I know all this is only possible through God by who we were both rescued, so I'm thankful we both can love each other in a way reserved for the few who accept this truth.

I'LL NEVER STOP

I'll never stop loving you, I will never abandon you, just love is all I do for me and you, I hope you have soft shoes to walk on the moon when you dream tonight in your room.

Blessed (bless-id), I'll see you tonight too, and bring a game of clue while we laugh the night away trying to guess who, I'll sing all the tunes that your mother forgot too because to me you're worth more than all the moons in a marble bag I got just for you.

Tonight you can little spoon while I hold onto you, so please don't move, because tonight, loving you is all I want to do, your eyes mirror a glow equal of a sapphire moon.

Making a more unique bloom is impossible to make, before you my heart felt half-baked, after you I found icing on my heart's cake, I feel like I can unfold my world into your airspace, your layers of depth are as vast as space.

I get scared when weightless; as you fill me with euphoria you replace my oxygen with, I'm afraid I might say something careless and I don't want to suffocate you with my presence, so when I back away just know I'm making sure your roots have enough room to be expansive.

For I would never want to dim what I found most attractive, most would for fear of losing a blessing that leaves others breathless but I'd rather you flourish than dim your spirit, if I lose you it was a pleasure loving you, but I hope, I'm the one you choose.

MOST ASK

Most ask "how are you not tired friend?" followed by the answer I always give: "she's my fire", "who?" they say, "the woman in my heart who sings to me through Robin's everyday".

They stare in dismay and walk away while I still have a smile on my face, waiting for that day when I finally see her face walking along softly with grace.

But it's not a race, because I want to work on myself until I'm her perfect ace, I won't chase, I'll let her set the pace and stand amazed I found her in this maze, whoever you are I can't wait to wait, I don't want to love you with only half of what I'm capable, let me set before you a full table of what I'm able.

When God unveils me to you I'll be someone from your favorite love fable, designed to love you a way that feels like we were weaved from the same cable, know that I'm traveling between worlds gathering materials for my soul so I can embody the man of which your deserving.

I would never want to be anything less than your perfect husband my darling.

ME AND ME

It's always this or that of why we can't pull the rabbit from the hat, didn't get where we're at by being a doormat, time to act before the lights cut to black and lose moments we both can't get back.

I'm not saying be a hellcat just don't be a house-cat, no sense being an idle wildcat especially if you want to live your ideal fantasy "Mr. Cash"

But what do you think will bring that? That's funny, something outside us bringing inner peace, what futility. Once you have something it's off to the next thing so you don't have to open the cellar underneath.

The air in that place makes it hard to breathe, dig deep, you'll find the answers you need and stumble into dark insights you allowed to shape your story that need revising.

Sometimes it's terrifying recognizing monsters have been crying for healing, begging you to stop the bleeding but most say "who? lil ol' me?", choosing victim mentality to evade responsibility of taking accountability.

It's not easy mastering your abilities but imagine if we never wrote this because we let fear dictate our story, you are beautifully made, please share your stories, and by the way

Good morning.

THE CROW

Out in a warm Meadow rests a doe thats the most beautiful in flow, not far behind follows a Crow who loves to watch her as she goes, hunters draw near, the Crow shouts "HERE"

She begins to glide in between the trees without fear, the hunters tried to get a bead on her but the Crow whispers "love is the answer", astonished at what the crow just said, one replied:

"Isn't that what God says?"

The other becomes angry with blood rushing to his head "IT'S JUST A STUPID BIRD MIMICKING WHAT SOMEONE SAID!!!", again taking aim he looks through the scope, holding his finger steady he holds his breath and his barrel begins to slow.

As he squeezes the trigger the Crow screams "NO!!!", the bullet that flew was caught by crow's chest bones, and as the Crow lie gasping his last; the man racks another round back, his son shouts "LET THE DOE GO DAD!!!"

the father looks at him with terrifying madness "WHY!?! It was dumb bird that got in the way of the firing line!", tears begin to fall from the son's eyes "That Crow was a sign... Killing won't bring back mom or heal that pain your feeling inside"

The man crumbles to the ground for the first time and roars an anguish that echoes through time, his son holds him as they both weep for the mother they lost yesterday night.

A DIAMOND

A diamond rests on a mound waiting to be found, everyday the sun beams down to shine the light on her beauty so her majesty abounds. The sun sees she's on an island with no one around, so to ensure she'll be found the sun moves all the stars in the sky around so a certain captain will land and find her in between the mounds.

One day an anchor drops down, a captain steps off the boat confused for a moment because he was sure he had the right coordinates, but the minute he looked through his scope he saw the most beautiful woman standing by some smoke, as he approached; the woman stood still, unaware of this man's intentions or hopes, throwing his hands up he says

"I believe I lost my way trying to sail back home, could you tell me where might I be, I know I have to be close"

She looks at him with the eyes of a ghost "my apologies, you just look like someone I know" curiosity peaked he asked sheepishly "who might that be my lady?", shaking with tears streaming down her cheeks she says:

"The man from my dreams"

WHEN I SAY

When I say I hope you're okay, I'm asking you to hold onto the promise of better days, treat your yourself sacred today because you've always been a blessing to everyone's day.

The ray you beam stays in strangers hearts for eternity, for that love weaves its way in between the seams of reality to manifest your dreams, you reap energy sown and in the coming days you'll have your mind blown with a loving harvest for your soul.

You'll soon realize it was never about the gold but the story yet to be told. Keep walking and don't you fold, your so close that all of heaven is watching in hope, there's a reason we're given the foresight of a microscope, so we have to lean on God's telescope.

If only you could grasp the full scope of the growth you've shown, it's like watching a lotus rise through the cracks in a muddy stone, despite your cracked heart and broken bones you rose as a Phoenix from the shadows alone.

Give yourself more honor because only you and God know what you did to survive the attacks you were under, each time you hit that floor, each time evil broke your core, each time death knocked on your door, your actions always said the same thing:

"I will push forward"

THOUGHTS

Thoughts can switch a stress response triggering cortisol, lowering immunity to almost none at all, do you know what happens to water when the vibrational word of love is called?

Beautiful crystals form like snowfall, our heart and mind is 73% water in all, that's how powerful your words are, enough to destroy castles and build temples, to me that's frag-mental.

One word can determine the state of someone's mental which

will rise or infect their spiritual visuals, so I'll keep spiritually visual and fight my downfalls per-usual.

The goal is not to act like a noodle when life's water begins to boil because how can you help your family if you crumble over every evil? I've noticed constructive thoughts lead to a problem that's quickly solved but emotionally panicked ones causes destruction for everyone involved.

Life is hard, but humanity only got this far by evolving through it all, imagine if our ancestors decided to take one day off, that could've lead to the whole tribe dying off, so if they had to struggle a hundred times harder than us then surely we can pick ourselves up and rise from the dust.

LOVE RABBITS

2 shy rabbits in school see each other and their hearts begin to bubble, they only chatted hopping along the burrow, as time flowed eventually the girl got married to another, "darn" thought the sir but smiled while giving cheerful words.

In a year, however, her groom got bored leaving her for a younger doe, the girl now alone heard of the sir's marriage through the corridors, "darn" thought girl as her heart began to burn.

In a year, however, his doe also left him for some youngster, sir now alone filled with sorrow thought only of the girl he once had eyes for, finally he said "I'M GOING TO GET HER!!!"

He ran so fast that below his feet was thunder; arriving at her burrow he thumped his foot ever harder, girl coming to the door said in awe "sir?", to which he stated "we were always supposed to be together! Would you still marry if I was your partner?"

As the words finally soared so did the love they always had for each other forevermore, and girl with happiness abounding in her mind throughout every corner with eyes watered said:

"OF COURSE I'LL MARRY YOU, YOU SILLY THUMPER!!!"

And they lived happily ever after.

HEAVEN IS HERE

A boy asked his teacher "where do souls go when they leave?", the wise man kneeled smiling "everything is energy and you're a piece of it connected through eternity"

"energy?" the boy asked curiously, "yes, the life inside and outside flowing through all things" the elder said chirpingly.

"So... one day I'll be leaving?" the boy asked uneased. "No" looking him in the eye with great certainty he said "you go back to the light on high to tell stories of how you did great things and laugh with your family who's already waiting because time is an illusionary thing"

The boy laughed "iLlUsIoNaRy", both laughing the teacher said "I love you son, now off to the beds!", the boy ran and jumped in, suddenly he peaked over the blanket in his bed

"Do you think we'll have wings when we're dead?", the father smiles while tilting his head "I don't know, but what I do know is you can ask God that question in dreamland, sleepyhead!"

Dozing off while yawning the boy says "ok, and while I'm there I'll also ask why he took me and mommy away from such a great daddy", the father murmured "what?"

Suddenly the man wakes up in a cold sweat, taking in heaving breaths; he grabs a picture of his wife and son and holds it tight to his chest and whispers

"I... know we're already together in heaven laughing about all this", tears falling on the picture as he says "because time is an iLlUsIoNaRy thing"

With a broken giggle he lays back in his bed... And he finally... Takes his final breath...

SPIRIT OF THE CROW

The Crow Is often seen as a sign of woe but is the most magical aerial shadow, a cape flows down the back exposing an artistic blue coat, which symbolizes transformation if you're looking for intuitive gold.

We see how cultures were impacted by this avian species, perceptions of them transition into different mystical means depending on the lens through which it's seen.

They remind us to live our lives in full and to let go when the divine takes control, to live in full because of the death they symbol, letting go because of the rebirth they offer.

Personally, I love the raven for its ominous nature to evoke a sense of memento mori; "remember that you must die" is undeniably the strongest sentiment that testifies:

"THIS IS THE WAY I LIVE MY LIFE!!!"

So the next time problems arise just remember when others go through the same hard times they just might look to you for a guiding light, so I ask you: what will they see?

Mediocrity or Perseverance during your time.

THE SCREEN

The sun beams weaving in between the trees dancing with the bees while roses blossom sweet dreams, little ones laughing while eating peaches with cream.

Robins are singing sweet melodies woven out of nature's loving being, magicians With endless magic in their sleeves while entertainers fire breathe.

The aroma of coffee gives more sweetness to every feeling, and the chips and cheese? Oh yeah, that's me.

Everything here feels like love is giving a hug with a tight squeeze yet in the distance you can see some still glued to their screens.

PARENTING?

I wish some parents would come back to reason, their kids are children for a reason and seek a loving figure to teach them, if they're not learning life from you then who's teaching? Eventually they'll associate the teacher for a mother or father. Many say:

"I LOVE THEM WITH ALL MY HEART!!!"

Yet their hearts find time for other things than their child's spark, silent abandonment leaves one of the deepest scars, alone in a room with nothing but a screen to keep them warm, is there any difference from that and them passing on? Physically there but emotionally gone, providing needs like a robot while they scream for attention which signals "LOVE ME MOM" and a pain that echoes "DAD, COME HOME".

But I understand, you have more important things to do than mending your child's broken heart.

PUT DOWN THE GUNS

This reality ties us together, a piece of me and a piece of you as we dance to the beats of what we want to see, between you and me unity is the answer for eternity.

For I would never want to see you bleed, I have faith these words will reach through fate to change our destiny, just believe with me and watch the divine shift the sea in favor of peace.

No need to keep loading magazines lying in wait for an imaginary enemy, the ones who oversee "our wellbeing" don't even send their children to do the things they send others to do joyfully.

It's an illusion that we're separate beings, there is beauty in trusting God blindly, unseen energy is holding everything together by a mind higher than ours and is veiled by majesty.

Trust there's no need for killing, remember your "enemies" are also God's offspring and it's up to us to realize these things so we can experience life fruitfully, like looking in a mirror, I love you family.

LIFE OF A NEW FRIEND

Ever since the 1st day we brought each other brighter days carrying our own internal weights, and today I just want to say you're the brother I wish I had on those dark weekdays when the world tried to take my light away.

I know there would have been more than sword play, I know you got your spooky ways but let little brother take the reins, I'd die a thousand deaths to see you okay.

I'll never walk away, even if you lose your brain, I'd still talk to you all the same while we laugh at finger paint and make hats out of paper mache, I hope I never have to throw you a birthday at your grave or play old videos at a eulogy about better days.

I pray for safety and divine intervention to help write the rest of your page, you and me will be connected forever through these pages on life's highway, and before I pass God's gate I'll say:

"Thanks for the brother you gave me since the very 1st day."

LOVE YOU

You are worth every loving word and deserving of every ward and much more, you are guarded from every sword, never will you lack anything anymore, for you are a creation to be adored.

Only open doors from this day forward, always remember the light that surrounds you pressing onward, only love will be your message with a bouquet of flowers.

Trumpets of angels blow in your favor, so I guess the only thing left to ask is: "is gold your favorite flavor?"

Because that would explain your pure heart that the divine loves to savor, your actions seem to emit a royal behavior, fitting for someone so humble and gathered.

Even if some may not see or understand why you carry this power just remember if it wasn't there they would be somber, they may whisper like children and act undisciplined, but only cause you give them space to be that way.

And if they're naturally a nutcase then you know they wouldn't last a day carrying the weight of the crown on your head that was rightly placed, never envy anyone still in that place from which you were saved.

Continue to thank God for the grace that you were chosen to be a leader through faith, truly you are worthy of soaring toward brighter days.

KINDNESS

3 wise men and a king are discussing the best way to bring down a dark Queen.

The 1st says "might is the only way I see"

The 2nd says "stealth is the only way I see"

The 3rd says "deception will get us in without keys"

The king replies to all 3:

"I don't want to lose any human beings"

They all stopped speaking as if they couldn't think, mumbling angrily "that is an impossible feat!"

Meanwhile a servant overhearing squeaked

"What if we gave food for their people to eat to show how much better their lives would be with our great king at the noble seat?"

The king's eyes filled with joy and joyous disbelief that such a wise man only sweeped.

He immediately fired the 3 while elevating the servant to the right hand of his seat because kindness is the only key to a kingdom of peace.

YOUNG LOVE IN THE SUN

A boy and a girl in their teens are running through the green "you'll never catch me!" she said gleefully, "my feelings already did!" the boy laughing.

As months went on so did the intimacy for each other's heartstrings, together they dreamed daily of all the adventures and romantic fantasies that could be conceived.

Then slowly each of them began realizing their words toward each other began to sound like honey, as years passed the love between them evolved into a sea.

Till one day he finally got enough money for the ring she wanted in her childhood fantasy, taking her to the beach of her dreams he got on one knee and said shakingly

"I love you, will you marry me?"

Overcome by a joy filled of great immensity her tears seemed to fall endlessly "of course I will baby", and looking back they both get the same butterflies every time they look at each other and say

"Do you remember the sunset that day?"

IS THIS YOU?

How could I have "worked" when I loved what I was doing more, the more time I poured into my art form it slowly started to twist and shift into different forms.

Thats when my soul's rose was born. Others finally began to recognize what God knew before it yielded fruit cores, my belief was the secret glue that held me through when the world used to reject what I do.

They tried pushing memories of their fallen fruits onto the character I was morphing into in hopes I'd give up too, but sweeter was the victory when my faith became true and pure joy came to.

I saw angels manifest my truth while instilling me with new found virtues, embodied only through the one who always remained true, even when I would move in ways I knew I shouldn't have moved He always said:

"I still love you"

After a while I started to look at myself with a faded smile cause how could I continue to say I loved him when I was doing the opposite of what he asked me to do.

He provided me with so much that I eventually gave up all the muck that was keeping me stuck, it was all he ever wanted me to drop, the thing about God is words don't matter but action does.

So if I'd kept on saying fluff to get stuff he'd know I was just another liar in the ruff, so although I gave up all the idols and pleasure pumps I could finally say:

"It's God I truly love"

LION AND THE SNAKE

A lion lays in the sun looking at the pride and reflecting on all he's done, a snake approaches and says "dear lion could I possibly be your consultant"

The Majestic giant replies "alright then, there is this snake problem by the water near our den; could you persuade them to move to a different location?"

"Of course!", the snake did exactly as he said and persuaded the others to go to the hyenas dens, "I've done it!" he said cheerfully

"Indeed you have, impressive deed" he turned his head back to his family, the snake confused asked "is there no reward for me?" to which the king looked upon him viciously

"The reward was the opportunity, also, now you know you are capable of many things and gained a sliver of favor with a great chief"

The serpent now angered snapped "I'LL TELL ALL THE SNAKES TO COME BACK!!!", to which the son laughed

"Father already told the hyenas a meal was coming before the day fell black"

MOTHER'S WORDS

Such wonderful words comes from a mother's love, so if you've never had one let me be the 1st one to say: you are loved, you are enough, you've always been more, you're always adored, you're never a chore to give these loving words straight to your one of a kind core.

How could I ever be bored pouring a love you've always deserved since your first morn, I love every star in your heart and the dark only magnifies their spark, so if you ever feel alone in your mental park, read this again and let my love be your ark.

I love you my superstar,

You've always been on the mark.

IF I WAS GOD

While playing in my thoughts I asked "what if I was God?" my left brain said "isn't that against the law?" while my right side said "we're the only ones up here and if we weren't supposed to prod, we wouldn't be here thinking it at all would we Mr. Law?"

So I laughed and jumped in the rabbit hole getting wonderfully lost. Well, 1st if I was alone I would split myself up into pieces and call it soul but eventually that would get boring and dull, so I would let bits of me perceive different realities with polar dualities to add opposing roles for depth of life as a whole.

But to be fair to me I would only let the other side touch the other if I put any energy into anything other than my loving being and I would make sure every dark action was compounding, I would be even more square by making personalized squares for each piece of me that wanted something different other than the intended unity as an experience you see.

Also I would put into place a law of reflecting to induce a state of: "whatever you do to me I get to do to you if I choose" to let myself in that self decide if I actually wanted to roll those dice really.

But in the end I'm just thinking, oh well, that was nice pondering on an infinite sea of possibilities with you dear reader right beside me.

TRUTH IN CHESS

There's truth in chess in the sense every piece is needed to move with a mechanical finesse, all you have to do is do your best and let the divine handle the rest.

Energy reads what's in the chest of every individual crest, just have faith in the universal scales of justice. So prince or princess; make sure you rest when deep down you know you're doing your best within your assigned test.

If you could just have anything right when you asked then there would be no sense of earned fulfillment, if you could go from being a knight to a bishop would you have the depth of character to sustain that position?

In that role it's not just the status but the expectation you'll maintain a noble disposition, you'd have to sacrifice all your time for knowledge so you don't accidentally give the wrong advice with good intentions.

Your influence could lead to the kingdom's fall because of your ignorance, so before you ask for higher positions ask yourself:

"Am I truly ready for a shift in responsibility and commitment?"

THE TREE WITHIN

Meditation takes your awareness to your soul's frequency, held together by a conscious intelligence beyond our current comprehending.

This piece of you manifests your understanding, breathtaking how God lets you create your own reality grounded in your created personality, letting you experience what you want to be in a sea of other entities.

Constantly shifting through vibrating states of reality to be here with me in the wholeness of knowing; uniquely loving others the way they need to be loved in the moment will elevate humanity.

And just like that you understand that love is the key to a joyous eternity entwined with the tree of harmony, I love you family. I wish everyone understood that without each other life loses meaning.

NO MORE WAR

No more war, we've seen enough to know we don't want anymore, deep in our cores we just want to open doors to the angels corridors, our hearts seek to find home by deciphering the map in humanity's bones.

Together united as one soul we are never alone, it's time to answer when God calls our phone, please speak to the fractured souls to let them know they aren't alone.

Behind their eyes we'll never know the lows they've taken to make them lose hope, they may have lost their family and couldn't cope, talk to them like a soul who has seen and felt more than they had too;

Remember what you went through? give the empathy you were shown, God could've left us in the snow but instead covered us with his cloak, please, help them home.

IT'S LIKE A GAME

1% better a day equals 365% better when you reach the end of the year's time frame, framing it this way shows growth in outstanding ways and you begin to look forward to better days.

Don't bind yourself to words you say, rather, get behind what you would rather display, it's all just a play anyways but the true question is: "what kind of being do you want to be everyday?"

What should you do when a darker version of you gets in your face? know that the reason you are put in a dark place is to be the candle in the darkest space, the divine knows you'll show the same grace that they've given you,

Their eternal ace.

ENERGY

Father and mother are elements contained within every soul's pendulum, the soul recognizes either side: masculine or feminine, begin to integrate the divine straight from the vines of this understanding;

That in creating love we manifest an evolved state of being, whereby loving yourself you start to love others and begin appreciating their gifts respectively, everyones connected, just living differently in a way of life fit for the way their vibrating.

I mean, what were you expecting in this ever expanding matrix of experience? It feels great to be alive with a law of reflection to tip the scales just right, it only makes sense to let everyone live their own lives,

How divine to state: "THIS IS MY LIFE"

I'M NOT ANGRY

I'm not angry just hungry for the life promised to me if I keep walking, seeing myself in a new light with a feeling that says

> *"I can't believe I was so lonely that I gave my feelings to people who used to make me feel lowly"*

Getting fiercely stronger every day, it's like my mind, body and soul are evolving day-by-day, I'm eternally grateful to the divine forces at play that are forging and tending my heart in these building days.

I just want to explode and show the world I'm great, but bigger hands are orchestrating this play and I have to remember not to rush anything that the master Baker said "don't move! At least not today"

So I guess I'll just have to wait and that's okay, there would be nothing worse than to come out half-baked, but I will say I must be a really SLOW bake because this waiting feels like a taunt from fate.

Which only throws butane on my will to continuously change, to stay the same would drive me insane because deep in my soul I feel a pulse of something great, even though others may not see the same I know it's only because they choose to ignore the beating coming from their own spirit's case.

While deep in thought about all this suddenly God pulls me out and says:

"You're ready, get after it"

THIS FIRE

The fire of inspiration runs red hot, inspiring to give more than what I've got, I keep thinking I've hit the golden pot but the point of the whole story is to let God lift me to my spot.

I'm just tired of washing pots and the universe knows my nerves are feeling shot, but every time spirit says "calm down hot shot just do your part and we'll lineup the shots"

Having faith the size of a seed isn't easy but getting me this far you better believe I'm holding onto my angels and I'm squeezing, I just can't shake this feeling that something only heaven can do will happen soon.

Blindfolded while holding onto a balloon knowing it's going to pop when it's time to, and when it pops I pray God won't let me fall but raise me up to a place on the rocks, either way I'm not going back to being lost, I'd rather walk in a holy fog than drift aimlessly on a self-serving log.

Devils will try to lead me astray as I get closer to the epilogue, but I know the difference between my Father's voice and a demonic dog's, keep walking on, and fear not, for we walk with God.

SECRET CLUB

One day all the wealthy children got together and said "what if we banded our wealth together to help the hungry and less fortunate?", all nodded but one asked "won't we need a philosophy and a special crest?", nodding in agreement they put their idea to the test.

Along the way their money began to take loss so one said "why don't we ask for donations as a small token for our efforts to help the rest?", so they began to take some and fill their chests, then the figureheads wound up with big play homes instead.

The poor children questioned "what happened to our home and food you promised way back then?" To which the brats now fat replied:

"What? You heathens really believed all that?"

Not funny how some places grounded in religion do that.

COMMUNITY

In the deep unconscious we feel for each other's grief, the energy at work is unseen and moves our soul to help our fellow beings, of course some may not be on the same leaf but the deepest part of them still craves compassion underneath, sometimes we're wrapped up in "me, me, me" that we forget without each other life would be miserable indeed, every kind deed plants a seed, when watered with care; it sprouts a divine tree where the branches intertwine with other trees.

To think it all started with you sowing a seed into just one human being, imagine if everyone could see the fruit from the love someone sown, truly it would ignite a warming fire in everyones soul, we may never get to know all the good that came from these gentle souls, but let's spread hope in honor of these great healers hopes for a world that's whole, you never know;

We could be one generous act away from heaven folks.

I SEE

I see some "healers" in the midst of healing themselves trying to lead the wounded, I see some using the broken to pump up their own tokens when they aren't even close to their own fulfillment.

It's better to heal yourself than listen to a hypocrite's hocus pocus, the "healing" they offer is often without experience and lacks empathy, it feels like someone trying to charge another's battery without energy.

Beware the wolf disguised in sheep's clothing, your spirit will provide the right questions that lead you to those who have pieces of answers, every great teacher has a variant of the same answer, they all say: "this is my understanding of the answer"

So it seems they mastered the art of being their own thinker, instead of letting others tell you how to think just read the source then be your own teacher, many hide this knowledge to stay in business through the ages but it all started with one soul who sat down to reflect "what do I think about these pages?"

so I'll ask you dear reader:

"Are you ready to stop walking aimless?"

HAPPY BIRTHDAY

Everyday is my birthday, a chance to reshape the gates of how grateful I am every single day, breath in my lungs, heart's a steady pace, really! What amazing grace! still have eyes to see when I'm tying my laces it really is the best day what great graces! not shaped by my yesterday's because if that was the case I'd be buying diapers by the cases! Erasing past mistakes by taking new action every way, evolving so fast if I stepped back it really would be doomsday, you're either love or hate but only one will get you through heaven's gate and if you're the one I think you are then Happy Birthday.

CROW AND THE PIGEONS

Pigeons are grazing in the field, not far, a crow sees this ordeal, "they have wings, they must be my people!" he said with zeal.

Flying over to them while landing the passel began Panicking "what is that dark thing?!", with blue glinting off his back he asked "what do you mean by that?", then a bird in the back jumped "don't play dumb why do you have those deathly wings you shadowy clump!?".

Still puzzling, he asked a different way "but you also have feathers, a beak and forked feet today?", the flock now angered finally said "you're not one of us! you resemble death!" with that they flew away quick as pests with a fellow raven landing in the same breath

"It's in their nature to be afraid of what they don't understand."

LETTING GO

The rarest kind of love is released when knowing that someone else can bring them deeper peace in what they're wanting, if you want one thing and they want every second of your time pouring onto their being what room do you have for your meaning? Is it worth discarding your highest-self for somebody else's insecurities?

If growth and love aren't the leading forces in steering a relationship's horses then of course both are sitting in a morgue of illusions where blame might start forming spiritual contusions which may burst an understanding that both have been using the other for a bouquet of pleasurable excuses for why they can't evolve acting clueless, wasting each other's priceless time, now that relationship is:

useless.

LOVE IS THE ANSWER

If love wasn't the answer then why does everyone hunger after it like a panther? It's taunted behind stained glass by holy ministers and some really do mean what they say which makes for a loving teacher.

However, true love is only found within, nothing outside of yourself can fix What's broken, one day you just commit to live your life different in order to get the dream most left. You're always connected with God, I mean, you're one of God's best. All you have to do is sit down and have a discussion, you might not like some of the answers, but hey, you asked the questions.

Your soul has one disposition that's geared toward wholeness, which means what's best for you and not your afflictions, It's okay to turn away from the asked corrections but you'll be right back because you'll get tired of fighting in the cycles of spiritual prisons, where you're the jailer and bondsman of your own dungeon, but this is life, so let's work on our reflection.

COSMIC DIAMOND

1 and 400 trillion is the cosmic estimation for you existing, So when another tries to pull your strings just remember how sacred you are in terms of living. Even the body will try to chemically control your independent thinking. It is puzzling; but if you dig deep enough consciously and merge with authenticity you begin to unravel mysteries that were once hidden by victim thinking.

Where thoughts go energy flows, so evolving is the only way to improve quality, it leads you to royalty while becoming the manifestor of your reality, don't be surprised when old "family" tries attaching to the abundant work you did internally, for once they drain your blessings, you go back to being nothing, the best defense against attacks like this is just the understanding they hold no power over you unless you give it willingly.

THE CLOCK

Think about this: what gives a clock purpose? if it wasn't for each piece's movement it couldn't function as a unit, in the same way a human would be semi-useless without another piece in their presence, this whole life at its essence is for the enjoyment of experiencing experience itself, to also connect and create our individual self, so I have a question:

What are you creating?

Since vibration is the source of everything created then it only makes sense that your words are manifesting what you're saying, it's worth debating. So let's watch what we say because you create daily, at least that's what I believe, know what I'm saying.

DEATH AND BUTTERFLIES

Such negativity and confusion revolves around death's teaching, The best interpretation would be a caterpillar transitioning to butterfly wings, the steps of growth from the old journey set the stage to transform into the butterfly when it's finally ready.

And that was just the beginning, so much deeper this truth speaks when you look even closer to the lessons Underneath, struggle from the cocoon allows the butterfly to get blood to each wing to prepare it for the harsh reality it will soon be facing.

Trying to assist this process will just rush the butterfly to a quick death but if left alone it will finally Spring, and when it does It's so happy to be representing its purpose for being.

All this to show that from struggling; you'll eventually be free to do what you've always wanted to do, just allow others to grow without you too, just do you, this is all death is inquiring, love you.

EXPECTATIONS

Whatever you do, lower expectation, putting too much energy into a situation or play-station will only bring more distress when looking outside of your vibration to Soothe abrasions that only God and you can heal through sacred discussions.

Sometimes life can be concussive which is why we need to work on our spiritual cursive to be more conscious of the blessings we have rather than cursing.

The health we have is somebody else's wish that's burning but we didn't even earn it. I'm grateful for that learning. It was given to us yet some take it for granted, no wonder every holy man is speaking perspective, and of course the women.

Now I'm no detective but if you found my whole poem defective because I put men before women in the line above then it's evident you're the one holding a jewel to the sun seeking imperfection, and that mindset is an infection which might need slight correction toward:

"What would happen if I looked for positive connection?"

CAN YOU SEE IT?

Can you see it in each person's eyes as they smile real bright? How the one they loved left this earth flying Into the night, or how hard they squeezed their hand as the life drained from their eyes?

Did you suddenly realize you can't see how much pain is behind anyone's eyes? Any smiles we give are testament to the light we hold inside that is held together by divine might. Why are we blind to individual lights and don't recognize each other's insights when without them we would only see blinds? Each of us gives a unique meaning to life allowing us to revolutionize our own minds within our own perception of what's right.

And through this realization I hope you see; without one another there is less reason for existing indeed.

TO THE NEXT GENERATION

I get up and wonder how much better I can be for the generation under, this life is like lightning but your legacy thunder, without you dear reader this whole message would be a blunder, what reason would I write this for If there wasn't another appreciating the creativity I pour? You are the whole reason I write this besides the need to express my soul-force.

Deep down we're all kids connected to the vine of the "divine", wordplay is fun isn't it? Don't let anyone tell you what's right because in the end It's all just subjective perception, just make sure your vision on life keeps adjusting.

Everyone has a unique meaning that shines bright but only they determine how high it will shine, in the lines above I said "you" 3 times so make a wish because you're the genie who can unlock your mind to get to your highest timeline, the angels told me to tell you that you're their favorite valentine, so keep your eyes up, you ray of sunshine.

THE ZEBRA

Is the zebra an animal with white or black stripes? It must depend on whose eyes and whose mind is looking right? In the same way; that's how they live their "life".

I use emphasis to bring attention that right and wrong are separated only by one's own perception, and mine is growth or destruction, without you reader, this poem would be a semi-pointless construction.

Only half a point because breathing is the blessing, you + God = your journey with the infinite. But remember without other reflections the walk in this 3rd dimension seems almost meaningless.

But like I said in the 49th word it's all a matter of individual perspective, so make sure you follow your own divine Internal directive,

you're called to be your highest self in God's ever growing collection.

THE YOUNG ELEPHANT

Out in the savanna a young elephant is feeling gloomy, he gets up, gets some water and says "good-morning", the sun begins to burn his skin so he sits in the shade of an acacia tree waiting for evening. "WHY ME!!!" he says painfully, tears streaking unbearably, but an elder monkey hears his wailing and asks:

"why are you crying?", "because the heat is burning, the water's dirty, my legs are swelling an-"

before he could utter another word the wise ape interrupted "WAIT!!! You have water? I know tribes that can't find any and their children suffer. You say each leg swells, well there's a sickly gazelle that wishes she had your health, and you say it's scorching yet there are animals still hiding in a worser hell. So I have a real question: do you have your parents? If you do, that's the biggest blessing, I say you're swell!!!."

The giant child stopped sniffling, understanding in his eyes as he began standing and said "your right, I'm sorry for acting like an ungrateful baby."

CHOCOLATE HEART

I see what others don't, your heart is made of Chocolate gold, most want to swish you around in their empty souls until the sweetness becomes bitter and cold from the lack of love within their own soul.

Stripping layers of your light to patch the dark holes they never healed to justify why they can't reach their goals, pulling you down the pole from elevating to under their control.

But I want you to know that if I ever had a chance to show you how far I would go to give your hand a hold, I hope you would call me when it is raining fire with the ground covered in liquid snow,

so there wouldn't be a doubt in your mind's folds that I would ever hurt you like the deadmen of old, when all you deserve is a lover that's the wrapper to your Chocolate heart and forever guards your divine soul.

DO NOT BEND

Don't do it... Don't you bend... you've finally reached a mindset where you know you're a God-send, when the vampires see this they will take it as a challenge to break your unbreakable spirit, realize that God will send another aligned with similar spirits.

And remember that evil will flatter thick as batter to cake the eyes from the intentions of what they're really after, which is control over your indomitable character, to have you surrender your power of soul to their cold coals of spiritual hunger

Too put you the disciple and whom you serve under for the accolade of "you were conquered", then they'll laugh with their fellow vipers that you believed their fake song of love they sung to you like the pied-piper, so make sure before any intimate encounter

Ask them: "so to which God did you surrender?", followed by examination of their mannerisms, showing where their heart truly lingers and will determine if at all that you might talk over coffee with a cube of sugar.

THE SPILL

When a child spills a liquid, 1st thing to understand is no yelling or you run the risk of reinforcing the belief "any mistake will result in verbal punishing" which evolves into a fearful misunderstanding of "never try new things because if you mess up, your guardians will cut you mercilessly.

Be the protector you needed as a child, where nurturing one's core and raising wisdom abounds instead of anger encased rounds that can ricochet around your child's crown inevitably pulling them down making it harder to get up when life knocks them to the ground.

Discipline with controlled punishment is sometimes needed but just a gentle reminder that the flowers you water in the garden of your child's mental eden will strengthen or weaken their spirit's inner being. Oh, and just one more thing before I leave, I have to ask:

"Are you ready to be your child's everything?"

THEY ARE ALSO A CHILD

100, 90, 80, 70, 60, 50, 40, 30, 20, even 10 are ages of man-made physical description, however, the real attention should be placed on one's spiritual inscription.

Wisdom flows through all and is indiscriminate of who wishes to be a seeker of her knowledge hidden within the walls of the infinite.

Blessed and guarded are the ones who say "just a few more seconds, almost finished"

for if you thirst after intelligence then the world will bend to the embodiment of Self-Evolution. From your brilliance births mental revolution.

Some may insult or try to pollute your intuition but only because they wish to justify their own spiritual dilution for sake of the one that stares back from a mirror of self-created illusions.

Now that's a true exploration of introspection, or at least my humble opinion.

I AM HOME

Wherever I walk alone with these bones of gold inscribed with spirit's golden tomes I understand that myself is the only being I control and call home.

It's not my place to put a ruler to choices others choose, they're just actions I no longer choose, rather I'm called to evolve and chisel myself with my own spiritual tools, many point and laugh together securely within an insecure group; justifying each other's insecurities as to why the pool feels better than the jacuzzi's whirlpool.

That's a party of fools, we're called to manifest our highest truths but most enjoy settling the minute they can lay down all day and satisfy their sweet tooth, I try to counter this gluttonous truth by continuing to make choices toward my evolution for deeper roots. Rooted in gratitude for getting to make healthy moves others wish everyday to come true, so with a stroke of luck I might've inspired the next healing guru, so to everyone offended: focus on you.

By the way, I'm a hypocritical man to, I just thought it'd be funny to offend the snowflakes in the room.

MIRROR OF MANNERS

Some believe others to be dumb and insert passive aggressive verbal hums then walk away mumbling with friends "they're so dumb", in response when I see an opportunity to lift them up.

I do, followed by my favorite one-liner hum: "I got you friend, any day under the sun!", shifting their internal dialogue to "what I said about them was wrong", deep down we all just want to be loved while being loved.

So when you see a fellow spirit trapped in egocentric mud you're called to show them our universal love that runs deeper than human blood, so show them your blinding light, unleash the flood.

I WOULDN'T

I don't believe Christ would pick up a magazine and destroy human Beings, so why listen to a suit rather than your savior's teachings.

How do you think God will handle a child taking a child's life? Little bit more than a belt and timing is always right, followed with a left straight through the mind's eye.

The Golden Rule absolutely applies especially since we're all experiencing different lives within the same cosmic vine, so when an ego-centered soul filled with self-indulgent pride tests your heart-line by telling you to bring them flatlines just remember whom you claim to serve and ask yourself:

"who am I more afraid of; a man in a suit or God's eyes?"

WE OWN NOTHING

I think of life like grabbing a handful of sand, the harder you run, the more grains slip through your hands, most enjoy rushing their Golden bands.

However, I noticed they use it to try and buy love which is the highest element in demand, spending their sands with someone who only wants the wallet in the back of their pants.

You can call this a cliché rant but the truth is:

if you felt reprimand then a piece of you might need healing chants, and if you're the one who chases money bands then you might want to feign poverty to see who will really help you stand.

But if you'd rather have an army of vampiric fans then ignore this letter of pen,

but I'd rather you be a lonely lion in your land than be around vamps filling their pig-pin.

THE ITCH

The itch feels like a candy-stick that flickers in the spirit, but soon after you're sitting on a bench wondering why you ever gave it a lick, It started out as "just a lick" which turned into eating the whole stick and now you feel sick, It's okay friend, I've been in that ditch, I just wanna say my hand is here if you ever need it, just reach for it.

I see the void your filling, I remember not feeling worthy of loving the soul looking back at me, your heart beats the same as me and you're more than worthy to stop hurting, so whenever you're ready I'll be here on this park bench waiting,

I love you family.

THE MONSTERS ARE CRYING

Deep inside my mind I found monsters crying

"Why are you crying?"

They looked at me with tears laughing

"We're dying", "No, it's death to living"

Their eyes filled with dread

"Why is it burning?", "we're purifying the wounds we lathered in self-pity".

They looked at me weeping

"We really do love you, we just didn't want to see you hurting"

Tears form as I hug them gently

"All of you did the best you could while I was growing, but I can't keep living in patterns of just coping",

I squeeze them closer bittersweetly, I murmur

"Thank you all for trying to save me when everyone else tried to break me."

Squeezing them tighter still, I yell

"THANK YOU ALL FOR STAYING WHEN THEY LEFT ME IN HELL!"

At that moment light started releasing from the wounds on their body, they suspended from the floor and before my eyes I watched them become the most beautiful canaries.

And still to this day they sing in my soul:

"We love you daddy!"

ALL IS ANALOGY

The best way to find more of your individuality creatively is to think about everything you see as an analogy, whether "scary" or funny, try to apply a new creative understanding for how an idea's frame could be used toward a more unique way of expressing your authenticity. Be a grateful soul who understands that 3-D is a blessing with the biggest being:

"I get to create my own personality".

Once you understand everything is a vibrating simulation, that's when you start to realize this matrix is activated through actions and willful intention, so if you want to be more creative then start shifting the dimensions of your perception.

HIGHER MOVIE

To better understand our existence and easier to Digest think of a pool of static and each piece is a vibration that shapes what you see, breathe, and feel. Thinking is just uploading dreams to the unseen realm to weave and create our own desired reel.

Your truth is home, so you choose the doors to open and roam, I recommend the one that stems from the 'One', but again it's your life so you do what's fun, everyone is sovereign and no one is wrong, it's merely a question of if you want to play along in someone else's home.

And if you do, doing so just surrenders your truth to another's truths despite being from the same spiritual cube.

So please be careful because not all of them love you.

POWER IS NOT ADDICTION

I know the feeling of release a drug brings. When you're so shattered that when death sings its enticing, it begins to have a jingle every time you hear the ring. I only escaped by the skin of my teeth and even now I'm almost in disbelief.

Secret was and is that I just wanted better for me, so when I thought about myself with no teeth, rotted skin and a mind blown to swiss cheese, I heard a voice inward scream "Leave! Never let these creatures get close again! PROMISE ME!!!".

In that moment I realized how rare a star I was; because when I looked around it was a galaxy of flies just chasing a buzz, they didn't care the button they were pressing was self-destruct, so I looked at one and said:

"You can have this, I'm done".

VAMPIRE FOR WISDOM

Everyone is craving something. Thirsting to quench a primal hunger that drums harder with every pulse of desire, most go after the control of another's power.

Siphoning one's powers to bend them to the curvature of what they believe life to be at the core of their desires. Which might entail you becoming a slave to a darkling's perverse picture.

Yet, only happens if you submit like a coward, and by doing so you accept the terms of being the lesser creature. On the other hand, you could thirst for the Golden Vein of Wisdom and drink from the Eternal Teacher

Leading to an everlasting fullness of soulful leisure, all you have to do is share the knowledge of the well by being a messenger for it's divine nature, so leave the vampire lessers and become:

"The Wisdom-thirsty Elder".

MOM?

I had a thought while pondering, why she had me while poor got me wondering, did my mother get pregnant for me or for her? Surely the question arose "can I afford my firstborn?".

However, as time flies I realize without the pain behind my eyes I wouldn't be able to relate to a single word or syllable I write, without my uniquely tailored struggle I would've never put pen to paper.

So the revelation is:

> *"to create a life grounded in passion you have to swallow the flames you agreed to before starting the mission".*

I love you mom and I'll still make sure your looked after, after all you did feed me and change my diapers, we also had the best laughter; but the way you act now I have to be careful you don't try to twist my character, I've worked too hard to love myself and I refuse to put myself through anymore hellfire.

Hopefully after all the help you'll go back to your loving self, I love you mom, please get well.

MY GRATITUDE

Seeing the pain inside of 3rd-world countries; I had a realization just how lucky and blessed my spirit is truly, for me to cry or complain would be an insult to those who are clawing to flee the hell they're in actively.

I show gratitude by turning my success into a race so one day I'll be able to help save the world from my own unique place in the "Clock of dreams we chase". Lifting weights, putting myself under the world's weight while I write despite jealousy's hate.

I march with the world on my shoulders toward heavens gates, the closer I get I feel my bones beginning to shake but I can't stop now especially since heaven is shouting

"YOU GOT THIS !!! DON'T LET OFF THE PACE !!!"

RIGHTEOUS ANGER

Trying to be ungrateful or spiteful around me will quickly lead to "re-evaluate your blessings."

Especially breathing, so many are crying while having a bed, food, warmth, and a loving family.

Meanwhile others are surrounded by man-made hellfire

praying for a coming savior. Don't come near me speaking self-pity while there are children starving.

Your "struggle" falls short in comparison to a child's suffering, so get out of my sight with your whining, do you have legs? Arms? Eyes? Even your healthy life?

Just reminding you of all the things you're taking for granted, so find peace in knowing that your problems are half a drop in an ocean of those truly haunted.

So hug your family and stop being a baby, be happy for your molehill problem hasn't shifted into a mountain sliding

"OH, I'm sorry... What is it you were saying again sweetie?"

DAD?

I open my eyes to find myself in bloody mud with death swimming in my blood, as I look around I see my son. Around him are demons salivating with thoughts of corrupting his soul; I try too move but my legs are broke.

I scream "SON OVER HERE", he begins to run but is immediately pinned as they hiss "look at your Father's sin, how can he save you? It's impossible to escape something so dense"

My Son screams "DADDY SAVE ME", as they began to drag him away; I feel my mind crack in front of my heart, a hateful rage began to swell, I hear my son again "DADDY PLEASE"

My bones begin to crack as I start to cry then laugh, my eyes roll back and black wings snap from my back, I hum "I'M

BACK". Before they could react I ripped out the kidnappers backs

They looked at me with disbelief and tried to run; but before a blink their legs were gone, a smile creeped across my face as I ripped into their lungs and at the point of insanity I heard a voice

"Dad?"

I NEVER WANTED

I never wanted you to hate me so, I only ever wanted you safe at home. You wish to live your life on your own I know, you're my family though; so why tell me about your snow knowing I'll want to clear the road?

It brings me pain to watch you drown in tearful rain, you walk toward me covered in bloody chains, what do you expect me to do? Just walk away? No, I love you to much; I don't play those games.

Whatever board you're playing on; I don't want to play, your wellbeing will always be 1st place. Call me a nutcase but I'd rather do what's right than lower you into a casket's case. Please understand, I can't lose you, my mind would crack out of place.

My heart races when yours paces, I know something is wrong before your face changes, before a single word reaches; or my eyes read a message I'm already at your door to guard you from any demons.

Truly, I hope you see, just how much; you really mean to me.

I WISH I WAS BETTER

I wish I was better, wish I could stop being a liar, wish I wasn't such a failure, I know the story isn't over, I will always push forward, I'm just tired of fear having the controller. I'm tired of demons and angels calling me a coward; knowing they're right from how I spend my hours.

I'm scared the voices might be right about the cross I bear "It's to heavy just leave it there" they laugh and stare. Yet, God sees something in me I can't see or hear. Trusting him is all I have left so even though I walk through the valley of the shadow of death; I fear no evil for thou art with me in every breath.

I know every breath could be my last, you'd think that'd be enough to keep me in class, it should be, so why do I still watch the clock tick past? I guess I don't feel worthy, sometimes I feel like my best days are behind me.

Wait a minute…

My feelings… They're lying to me!!! Logically, if I keep going I'll make my dream a reality. I've seen it happen for others off worse, so why not me? Why wouldn't God open those doors? I know they'll open when He says "you're ready" so I'm done being sad about my heading.

Because in the end; It was all about trusting God from the very beginning.

I CAN'T

I can't live like this anymore, wasting time for fear of imagined horror, fears that I can't maintain the sword given by my lord. Lead by a heart drenched in hurt to "protect" me from anymore shameful dirt. A deep part still believes I am my scars, yet even deeper I know a butterfly forms in a caterpillar's heart.

It's a choice: to drown or listen to the noise. It may feel as if you have no voice; like you're being melted into a mold to become God's toy. Yet, our way made us broke in the 1st place, once a beautiful vase, our decisions shattered us into a disgrace. We can't play coy; it's growth we're trying to avoid.

We're slave to one or the other; but only one side cares for you like a Father, loves you like a son or daughter, pushes you toward better for the sake of His character, for we're sired from truth; not a liar. He offers us a place in the empire while asking our surrender, to live and conduct ourselves like we are His mirror.

Who knows what's best for us more than our creator? Who knows better on how to get us our desired character? Who other than the Maker of water and fire could actually make our souls flower? I've made up my mind; I choose to walk with my Father, I'm done being a coward,

But most of all I'm done hiding in the devil's liquor.

HAVE I GONE MAD?

Things that once made me happy are now the cause of my suffering, smoke steals my vitality and drinking destroys my sanity. Things I once indulged; I find are turning my body to mulch. Places I once found joy; I find are full of people that just make noise. "Have I Gone Mad?" Or was I born into a world that calls good "bad"?

Being surrounded by opinions painted as facts will give your perspective cataracts, and when you stop dancing to the masses playbacks you're made the outcast for wanting to make your own track. I found this is the right of passage for those who don't just want to be a match but a blazing beacon for other "Mad-Cats".

This life is ours and how we spend our hours is for our own story we wish to flower. Many a year from now our family won't remember us for even an hour, they'll be focused on their own timer. So be everything you ever wanted to see, do everything you ever wanted to achieve, because life is like the falling of leaves, so ride the wind while you're still green and always remember:

"All things are possible to him that believes "
— JESUS CHRIST

WHY ME?

"Why Me?" I used to scream, yet now I see "Why not me?". Just like all others; I deserve to suffer, I fall short of God's intended order, sometimes a listener; sometimes a liar. I know pain is the only way God is able to pull us closer, so when I'm put in a fire I just whisper:

"I understand Father"

Whether I lose a family member or my health becomes shorter; I know I deserve the executioner. If it wasn't supposed to happen then it wouldn't have, if it happened then I'm grateful it wasn't worse then it could have, when the devil laughs it's because he knows God makes good from bad.

It's nothing personal, it's just business, to tempt you away from looking at your situation through God's vision. It's not about us; It's about the mission, to give reverence to God in any season for the gift of breathing, only by harmonizing to His symphony can we find harmony.

All this is easier said than done; but this is how you weave peace from any madness spun.

WHY DO YOU LOVE ME?

Why?

I'm full of lies, I've damaged my mind, I treat the body you gave me like a pigsty; so tell me why? Why do you waste your time on fixing my life? Knowing my dark ties to the other side you still try to bring me to life with tears in your eyes, I don't understand… Why?

You're cloaked in light, you are the Son of the Most High, I've rejected your voice to many times, I deserve lashes for wasting your time, what could you possibly see when you look into my eyes? Holding me like you found a beautiful jewel, please tell me: why do you love a fool?

I guess it's cause your essence gives me breath, I guess you see your child who just makes a mess with all the amazing gifts you give from your chest. Loving me like this gos beyond words I can express, you ask me to show gratitude by doing what your Son said, to which I say:

I will do my very best.

MAN & WIFE

Man is made for law and logic, you see it in the biological makeup, that man is strength and protection, that he finds the answers to a question, there is no question he picks the direction, it's something that was built in, It's life's way of saying "This one will carry the burden".

It doesn't mean to be a tyrant, it means standing on the best solution and requiring your family to trust it. Meaning there's no room for ignorance, or you could starve your family by accident. Much responsibility means you need to be in peak ability; to just feed your family.

A wife is the light in a man's life, she holds him through his darkest nights, she cleans out the darkness in his mind, for she knows the cost of the battles he fights. She fills his spirit with words of gold to remind him why she gave him a part of her soul, now I have to ask:

Isn't this the perfect balance between roles?

THAT NIGHT

I remember the night I sealed a letter with the tears I cried, discarded by my wife I wanted to take my own life; but instead tucked a cross into the folds of a letter detailing my desired life. Called crazy for my sudden connection to light I was divorced and left out to dry.

It was like something out of a book, I begged God for a second look, I weeped for Him to rewrite my book, for the story I was writing I knew would lead to a hook. If I told you what followed after; you'd bury me in laughter "The crazy adventures of a 4-time-homeless-soldier".

I was placed into a spiritual blender, all my fleshly desires became physical matter, revealing temporary pleasure is really a snare to keep me buried in addiction and fear-made-batter. Over and over I repeated my mistakes until I finally learned that which I was supposed to learn:

To put my purpose first; over a world that would watch me burn.

NO MORE!!!

NO MORE!!! No more self-induced sadness to justify lack of action, no more meditating on the blackness to slow traction, no more disguising laziness as "planning for action", no more crying over those who left me in trenches still healing from stitches, I'm ripping off all the leeches!

I know I'm capable, I know I'm able, I know I'm a knight of the round table. I know many pray for me to crumble; but to do so would insult my savior. I'm called to be humble and let my actions rumble, I could care less about bitter souls that grumble, I fight for the ones still buried in the devil's rubble.

"Who do you think you are?" You ask, I'm a deadman who was brought back!!! I'm the one from alleys black at whom they used to laugh!!! The madness in which I was drowning taught me to climb my mountain, listening to great minds is how I received the gift of reason while Christ alone expelled from me the demons named "legion".

And so now I know:

Only God; can bring me home.

GET UP

Can you see it? Beautiful isn't it? How a loving spirit can lift us from a pit, how they resist darkness to show us a better way to live. I doubt even with imagination we could fathom their torment, how much pain has to be felt to say "I won't let anyone else feel this way"?

What kind of person would sacrifice their own heart to help heal the broken? Must be one of God's children. That's the only answer I can reason why a suffer-stricken soul would love others without reason, even bleeding they'll stitch you before their own stitching.

It's bewitching to see them hugging ones still in ditches, through them we see the world God intended, that love is what drives me up the mountain, if they can turn suffering into compassion then I can craft passion from sadness. If they can do it then I can to,

I'm getting up because of what I saw you do.

Thank You

PAINS OF PROGRESS

It swims under the skin, the cause for every sin, an animal within that wants dominion over the light that's God given. We pick the fruit that's lowest for the same reason we delay progress, it's easiest. Years of human evolution produced a body to produce, eat, and avoid dangerous situations.

This is why great people praise discipline, they found out you can change its condition by forming habits that ground you into your desired version, it's the hardest thing to do when your broken from all the love you've given. So used to giving your heart to everyone you forgot how to be someone.

Trauma in the body isn't uprooted easily, it feels like whole parts of you are dying, which is good, it's cleaning the wound so the medicine can heal through, I hope these words helped you, I know how much the process rips at you, but please...

Don't go, we need you.

I'M NOT OKAY

I'm not okay… Smile on my face, I'll hug you while I break, it hurts to be the same, I need to change, as I rip at the chains my skin also rips away. I no longer want fame, I no longer wish for a gold chain, I wish for a better me that doesn't act insane, I wish for a heart that isn't the devil's slave.

Suicide promises no more growing pains, yet, I would never say that's the answer to someone half my age. Why is that? Why tell someone else to act other than how I act? Perhaps, I know life isn't a trap but something that's gift wrapped, maybe the old me is just trying to keep me trapped.

Either way I can't go back, the pain is to great to stay cracked, looking back at myself I can't even laugh, I just think "wow, all that time went to the trash for people who treated me like trash". I learned:

I tolerated what I thought I deserved, which caused me to be treated less than I deserved.

But no more, I know my worth.

I WENT MAD

Thrown to wolves

I was such a fool,

Crying in a bloody pool

For one I called my jewel.

Didn't have much money

Always was someone clumsy,

They were the 1st one to say:

"Hey baby, you look lovely"

Latched on like she was the last one,

Opened my heart with the cast still on,

Fresh from heartbreak I wanted love,

Abandoned; I craved touch from anyone.

But once both of us were healed enough

I started to see how my other wasn't enough,

There was always something for why I couldn't be happy,

I find out peace meant growing; and love meant sacrificing.

Doubts dressed as questions came for reflection

"Are they worth my transformation?"

"Do they really love me beyond comprehension?"

For if they left I would feel like it was all for nothing.

Which begs the question:

Why do I "need" somebody to be somebody?

Silent reflection

KIDS RAISING KIDS

Most grow in broken homes,

As kids raise their kids

They treat them like old bones,

Embedding in them faulty code.

Leaving them at home they go drink till their mind explodes

Wasting time with strangers who just want sex and blow.

A piece of them sits at home waiting for mom to come home,

Hoping daddy will bring back the movie he promised to show.

As the child gets older they get used by monsters,

For the creatures were their only "loving" figures.

Older still, now they have triggers from trauma that lingers.

Searching forever; for a mother and father in the broken hearts of strangers.

Is this really what you want for your sons and daughters?

THE WALLS COME DOWN

You have to feel it… the pain welling up has reached the ceiling.

You can't hide it no more, it's at your core, it's rattling your door.

Let it hurt, let the anger spurt, the tears are a promise you won't break your word.

Let the walls fall forward, let the lies crumble, let your heart rumble, Let the old you be toppled.

Let the pieces fall all around, it's okay to no longer be the clown.

It's time to make yourself happy now, time to wear your crown.

Leave the madhouse to the ones who want to stay down, be proud,

You could've drowned in the sickness many still swim around.

I'm proud of you… I mean every letter to, I'm excited for future you.

Remember, every step is proof you're no longer a fool, don't let the devil trick you!

Even if you fall, the progress didn't go away at all, it's a lie to keep you in nightfall,

You answered the devil's call one time; but you used to answer all the time.

Don't let the king of flies turn you back into a lie.

"LOST"

I walk through my house of glass,

Wanting all of it to burn and crash,

There is no love in this empty cash,

Why did I chase this? All this trash?

No one to share. No one to care. No one. to hold dear.

Wounded laughter and old pictures are my only visitors,

Only one doesn't ask for a favor, says hi every hour,

What would I do without him, "The Man In The Mirror".

No, I don't want a drink. No, I don't want a body under my bedsheets.

All sensations a human can chase turns one to a corpse with a "happy" face.

My only joy is when I push past "the broken little boy", creating light from void.

What irony, that what I became pushes them away, I forget they prefer their grave over change.

Is this why I'm alone?

Is this why no one calls my phone?

Is this why I have an empty home?

Is this why so many belittle my soul?

Because I grow?

HERE I AM

Here I am, finally on my knees, just one squeeze, and I'll have peace.

"No… Please… Don't squeeze… They need you… These lost babies…"

The barrel's already in my face, if I don't pull; I'll just be a disgrace.

"It's disgraceful saying your brave for letting death take you away"

I CAN'T DO ANYTHING RIGHT!!! WHY SHOULD I FIGHT!!!

"Fight for the coming light, it can't rain all night, live for your wife"

Who would ever want to be with me? I don't even have belief in me.

"Not now maybe, but if you keep healing, you'll attract a queen that loves you dearly"

Why not love me now? Why can't she love me when I'm down?

"The way you think, the way you drink, do you think it's fair for her to also sink?"

I… NEED… Somebody…

"You need you more badly than anybody, you can't love them right without loving yourself properly."

So what you're saying is…

> *"Become who you want to spend the rest of*
> *your life with through eternity"*

IN THE SILENCE

Locked behind walls of shadow, they think I don't know.

The smiles are just for show, their heart inside rots slow.

Afraid to let go of the bliss that brings about death's kiss

They drown in blackness laughing while consuming madness.

Believing this is all they'll ever be: "A mistake dressed as a human being".

Never searching for how to be; but looking for reasons to play hide-and-seek.

Wants to have everything but doesn't want the responsibility.

Yet, in the silence of forgotten dreams their calling rips at their peace.

The most inner-self knows thyself,

Depression comes from lying to yourself,

It's the soul's way of crying for oneself,

It's a call to bring forth your highest self.

Please… Quit trying to kill the purpose of self.

DEMONS IN MY HEAD

I'm not worthy, a sinner, filthy.

Sometimes wishing death

Trapped inside my depth,

It's painful drawing breath.

I scream in my bed,

It's change or death,

And most the time;

I'd rather be dead.

I know what they don't,

We're supposed to grow,

So when I'm down below,

I'm reminded sulking is a joke.

Demons gnaw on my bones.

Angels mock me with words I've sown.

Verbally whipping myself to force growth.

I mean, what else am I going to do?

Hide until I'm 6-feet below?

THE GAMES

I understand, the games are a wonderland, an escape from the pains of being superman. It's okay, we're more than just a part in an engine, to be a kid again, even for just a minute, is heaven.

Don't hate yourself for taking a break from hell, just don't fall in the well. Growing doesn't just help you, it inspires everyone around you, "if they can do it then I can to" is much better than accepting to lose.

It reveals just what humanity can do, and to think; all this hope will come through you doing what you're called to do. It follows you, it haunts you, it wants you, you watch the art others do; because it's a part of you.

Don't fight what is your birthright, everyone starts out a little less bright. It's the right of passage to separate plastic from vintage, keep harvesting what makes you authentic, only then will you find happiness.

DECAYING HEART

Gone, the smiles of summer days.

Love, no longer a childish game.

Searching, for someone to claim.

Hoping, to die with them someday.

Comparing ourselves to yesterday

We brand ourselves with mistakes,

Crippling our hearts with shame

Saying "I deserve the scraps given day-to-day".

You are what you think, you think what you are,

So be who you are. Look at yourself and ask:

"Is the life I live trash?", If so, why continue the path?

A decaying heart will start to call good "bad"

For the same reason it started to go bad:

To keep living in a dreamland gone bad.

A REAL MAN

What is a man without his core?

What is a man without his sword?

What is a man without his anger?

What is a man without his wrath for monsters?

How can a man be a father if he isn't a warrior?

How can he protect his family's future if he's a coward?

What will he do if his wife and children are in danger?

Is it safe to say nothing? How can a weak man save anything?

He can't, many families perish from a man being cowardly,

This is why it's important to get your own role in order

Before thinking about carrying a woman and kids on your shoulder.

I mean, who wants a weak-willed father? No one, that's the whole point brother.

THEY BRAINWASHED US

The mind is rewarded by completion of a task, the wealthy class found a way to highjack this biological process, algorithms designed to keep us in a state of mindless laughs while subconsciously reprograming our life's map.

They want you to forget, they want you to spend, they want you in a cycle of mindless consumption. Feeding you chemicals and additives to destroy your ambition laughing at how "easy it is to control the masses".

Marketing what brings sickness with fitness; they make billions off the diseases we put in our system all because we saw someone "more worthy" do the same thing. What happened to us, aren't we also human?

How did they brainwash us into believing we're nothing; when without us they would have nothing?

THE TWO BROTHERS

There are two brothers, they both hate the way the other sows, one is focused on growth while the other stays below, one day they argue almost coming to blows. "Why do you drink away your purse?" Says the first, "for the same reason you invest yours" the other snaps with bitter words "I enjoy it, life is more enjoyable when you can forget your troubles".

"What about your family? Don't they deserve a life that's care-free?", "my family is happier to have daddy at home playing with the babies" the second smiling. "What if something happens and you can't afford to save them?", "then I'll find a way to get the money in sum", the first gives a disappointing look "but brother, why not work harder to save them from future hooks?"

The other's anger boils over "YOU SLAVE ALL DAY!!! Just to wind up away from the same family that wants you to stay! All that money and comfort for what? You can't give your children love while tilling through mud! I love holding my daughter, and I love teaching my son! I'll be damned if someone else raises my little ones!!!",

"At least I can give them whatever they want" says the first,

"Everything except your time, which is more precious than your gifts of dirt."

Says the other with bitter words

THE DOUBTS

I say I love you,

Yet, if I loved another how I love you; I'd leave me too,

You did more than you had to, still, I lie to you,

You pulled me from the deepest pits of "you know who",

I'm sorry I believe in my past mistakes more than you.

But If I was sorry really; I'd leap in joy for the position you promised me,

I wouldn't look back, I'd stay on track, I'd work so hard that I'd break my back.

The devil in me laughs, so certain he has me had, going all in on: "he'll drink that glass"

Only you see something they don't, Only you are willing to go broke for a man labeled a joke.

Why do I hide?

Why do I lie?

Why am I still alive?

Why God, waste your time?

I understand however,

You say "forward", I stay a coward,

So what else can you do? Other than

Let me wallow in my tower.

Maybe you won't leave,

But I would if I was given what you receive,

But that's why you're God and I'm just…

A piece of meat.

ONE DAY

One day I won't hate myself, One day I'll look back and wish I asked for help, One day I'll be able to love myself well instead of leaving my soul covered in welts, I'll probably cry from the way I gave myself hell, forever hiding in my shell.

Watching my mind melt in the flames of depression I casted on myself, knowing only love can break the spell. My past is a bottomless well the angels say I shouldn't dwell.

Yet, I yell "ALL THE EVIDENCE SAYS I'M UNWELL", to which God says: "My son, the old has been expelled, come, live the life I blended for you on my pastel". Climbing up the stairwell I find it hard to say farewell.

Yet, this is what I asked for,

This revival

THEY DON'T WANT YOU

They don't want you, they want what comes from being with you.

The status, the access, just a tool to piggyback to their own success.

Laughing at all your jokes, really believing you're an ignorant joke.

That you're to naive to see they're after the benefits of being in your company.

"I'm your ride or die" I've heard an absurd amount of times.

Yet "they're different" right? Many lie to save their own life,

So why wouldn't they promise "gold" to get back tenfold?

Love means you give, love is actions, be careful who you let in.

Remember, even Judas tried to hide his true intentions,

You'll be a "villain" when others can't use you as leverage

To shortcut blessings that are only had after the pilgrimage,

Don't rob the children of their own journey with the infinite.

Let them hate you for living a life with God in obedience.

HOW GOD SAVED ME

I was dead, lost on a world I made inside my head. Unable to see all the demons that took root in my family tree or how deep they buried themselves in me. Identity weaved from a family who gave up on their dreams, just a kid, at the mercy of others broken beliefs.

So when I finally married I settled for my high-school sweetie, who turned out to be just as cracked as me, a toxic love indeed, we fed each other our wounded pieces; no surprise when I cheated.

No father in the picture, I had a spine of copper "she wants to beat me? I'll get love elsewhere". I feared divorce, afraid of being seen as an idiot by my peers I kept everything a secret between my ears.

Everything only got worse, the abuse took its course, lost a career from the lies she murmured, of course. Then, finally, the grand finale: The Divorce. My heart had taken a drastic turn when I begged God to take away my soul's heartburn.

I was labeled "crazy" for my radical love to my new lord that I was discarded and left outdoors, looking for shelter; my dysfunctional family left me to the natural order, begging my ex-wife, she left me in my darkest hour.

Father to our son mattered none, she only cared about "who he was". I was taken in by a co-worker from the before months, gave me enough time to get my own truck, found a job making double what I've usually done, what great luck.

Saved a woman from an abusive family of narcissistic humans and to be honest I thought she was the one God had chosen. Yet, just like the last, problems again, started to come back, and after herniating my back she went right back to the family who treated her like trash.

Homeless again, I went to the hospital for help on my condition, Christ sent angels dressed as humans to help me get movement, I never gave up faith God would lift me from the devil's pollution, and he did, a disability check signed: Remember the Mission.

But I didn't, I wasted it on booze and women, toxic relations, and situations I should never have been in, once being used by the world like a toilet and devolving into something less than human

God hugged me and said:

"Come back son, you are forgiven."

DON'T GIVE UP ON ME

Father, don't leave me, I'm at war with the enemy inside me. The past pounds like hellfire rounds, I'm still adjusting to being a warrior now, I'm still learning to be proud that in Christ I have been found. I can't lie, I'm scared to die, I'm afraid of this cleansing light.

As the broken child sheds away; I feel a deep sense of pain, this was a mold I created to keep me "safe", a mixture of what others had to say and a dash of my own clay, it's hard to say goodbye to a version who got me through my darkest days.

Yet, it's time to put away the childish ways, time to accept it was really you who brought me through, time live in the truth of growing closer to you. In order to know myself; I have to surrender to self, I love you Dad, please, help.

I'm not well, only you can guide me out of hell, I confess you are the truth and the life, please God, remove from my back all these knives. I'm barely standing from all the attacks on my life, Please God, in your Son's name, this prayer, I write.

THE VENDETTA

I don't need to do anything, what God can do is so much worse than what we can conceive. He controls time's current, at the perfect moment; their whole life will crumble in moments, while God mourns over his child who brought upon themselves their own destruction.

A path chosen by their own actions, a road he begged them not to travel, for He knew what was going to unravel, the wrath to be had when a parent finds their children abusing an innocent child, He is perfect in all things, including justice; forgetting nothing, everything is filed.

So when it comes to revenge, leave that to whom all matter bends. This isn't a movie, leave it to the judge of humanity, The One above all things. Or, be caught in the same wrath by disobeying how you're called you to act, forgive them, that's all He asks.

I'D MISS YOU ;

Wait...

Let me talk to you a moment, I noticed you've been going in the basement, I see in your eyes the dissonance. Feeling your worth comes from your circumstantial birth. "You're an accident" slips from the lips of the broken reveling in ignorance. Unable to see the importance of a growing tree, blindly hurting anyone for the pain they carry.

You hide from the mirror like it's your worst horror, like a doubtful artist who hasn't finished their sculpture, do you know what happens when the most wounded soldier becomes a healer? They save others from the cellar they used to be trapped under, they give them a guiding fire to fight off the many monsters, helping the forgotten become warriors.

When the pain has reached a critical stage; only you can choose how to write the next page, either "how I fell" or "how I broke the spell" choices that refine you into an animal or a recovering angel, no one gets a say in if you stay unwell. You are the master of your soul, so tell me; what will you do when the devil has you in a chokehold?

YOU DON'T WANT ME

Most women only want one thing, the better half of the man they marry, they fall in love with the version he displayed like a fantasy, men do this for one of two things, to get them under sheets; or to show his ability to achieve, biologically proving he's worth loving.

The HCMST survey finds about 70% of women initiate divorce. In America, odds of a full marriage are half a score, 50/50 are the chances of a man's world crashing to the floor, they say "love is the only thing I came for" then wind up leaving with over half of what the man worked for.

Brother to brother, say "prenup" and see if she's bothered, after all, it's just an agreement that sets the boundaries if it all falls over. Why not protect yourself; from one who might only want the gold for herself. Marriage can be a legal hell, please, don't leave what I said on the bookshelf.

WHY WE'RE AFRAID OF LOVE

What's my greatest fear? Why loving you; of course my dear, the only force that forces you to chart the hardest course. All life is held into frame by the maker of this mainframe, only love would do such a thing, only God displays the true essence of what we can only name. Giving all He is; in complete service, so we can feel what it is to live with purpose.

To love means to follow his blueprint, it means giving all of myself to give you the best experience, it means to be vulnerable and share secrets; so we can have an intimate relationship. It means leaving myself wide open for the pain of abandonment; and understanding you'd only leave if you felt me inadequate.

Yet this is why we love ourselves first, God does; and that's why the cosmos doesn't burst, He loves what He does for us despite the minimal worship He gets from us. So I need to know if you're the one, for if I'm going to love, I'm giving all of myself, not just the crumbs.

HOW LONG!!!

HOW LONG!!!

Have you kept me locked behind bars!

The warrior inside that carries our spark!

Fire of the heart I refuse bending to the dark!

Think not, give everything you got!

Blood runs red hot, eyes are bloodshot!

The past; lessons learned, the future; passion burns!

You say gardener; but our heart is a warrior!

LET ME RAGE!!!

BREAK THE CAGE!!!

TAKE BACK THE PEN

AND WRITE THE PAGE!!!

NO LONGER

No longer do I belong to the devil's order.

God commands me to walk in power.

Buried the old for new to rise from under.

CALL ME A COWARD!!!

I'll smash your head between a door before another word uttered!!!

You'll be left in shock from the butt-end of my wood-stock!!!

Thought is was your time; but you're on my clock!!!

Lights off as the monster caves your skull with a rock!!!

Right or wrong, I'll die ripping your head off!!!

THREATENING MY FAMILY!!!

When they find your they'll think a wendigo shredded your body

And I'll be 1000 miles away from the scene where I left you buried!

Now to me "that's a funny story".

I WAS SAVED

Covered in fire, trapped in lies strong as barbwire

Thinking "no one is looking for a coward".

Condemned by my own judgement

Wishing I could redo every moment.

Suddenly the sky opened wide and out shined a bright light,

A hand pierced through the veil of night "my child, you are mine".

"Never were you forgotten, never were you unguarded, come back to the garden".

Rising from my coffin; devils sunk their claws in "It's a trap! He offers only eternal hardship!!!"

"IT'S BETTER THAN WASTING AWAY IN DARKNESS!!!"

As I reach for my king's garment they pull me back with a harness of lies I've identified with.

I weeped "Father! save me please!!!" drained almost empty, I reached for his hand like a lost baby.

When He came near the demons ran in fear, and as I lay broken; He hugged me close and whispered in my ear:

"I would never leave you here"

EVERYONE'S A SKELETON

Under skin deep; rests one's being.

Beneath all the meat; is a soul underneath.

A collector of moments, but here lies the real question:

How do they interpret the good, the bad, and the friction?

What actions do they take? Do they mirror what you want to emulate?

Do they grow through pain? Or do they crumble for pity's sake?

In the end, is being with them going to water or hurt your faith

For the world you're seeking to make? A pretty face doesn't mean their heart's a peaceful place.

Stop trying to make them fit into a frame your imagination made,

Don't make excuses for the parts that leak through their inner gate,

Believe in the fruits displayed not the beautiful words they say.

Don't let your heart be lead the wrong direction for a beauty that's skin deep and doesn't reflect their true intention.

Remember, that in the end

We're all just skeletons.

So go for their character,

For salt also looks like sugar.

GOD FIRST

He gave me this chance, He let me take you to the dance, He said "this is my daughter, be a man". Taking his hands; he removed the strands that belonged to the shadow-lands, And with his eyes; He destroyed my pride, preparing me to enter your life with the right mind at the right time, God is good all the time.

Thank you God for showing me the light, thank you for showing me the truth of the night, that it only seeks to destroy your potential in life, that it trades instant joy for pieces of your mind and kills your soul in exchange for a "high". My God, thank you for guiding me out of the fog that sought to turn me into a frog.

Once lost, now found, forever bending my knee to the one true crown, once a clown, now a knight proud, I will bring the kingdom of my Lord to this ground. This is the vision I want see before I leave: every soul receiving Christ as their King, for only through seeking He; did I find my purpose to be.

THEY WOULD'VE BROKE YOU

I want you to understand, some can't go where you can, so to save you from long term suffrage at the enemies hands they were removed at a level of pain you can still withstand. For if they stayed a second longer then what was had; your very heart would've gone mad. Be glad that God always has your back, or else you would've died from a heart attack.

The kind of person you are deep in the heart is why your protected so hard, don't look at what happened as something so dark, you were saved from greater scars, please understand, you're a man of hearts, you were guarded from a false love's brutal marks, ones where they may have altered your spark.

Your light is to important to be corrupted by night, legions of angels have pulled every string through time to ensure you'll reach your highest form of life. It all happened for your good, remember, be grateful you were saved from a love that would've chopped you in half like firewood.

WHY SUICIDE?

Thoughts of suicide come from trying to become someone, when one realizes growing is the only thing worth doing under the sun they finally feel the weight of all the wasted time they've spun. And the seeds they've sown in their mind are not simply undone, they must harvest it up for new seeds to be planted and sprung, they do this by wrestling against themselves for what they've done.

They begin emotionally reconditioning themselves that the old way was actually hell, some of them can't handle the shame of admitting they were drinking from a poisonous well, so they choose to stay unwell for the pride of "I know myself". Yet, deep inside they know their path is made of death and lies, causing a cycle of depression throughout their life.

The longer they wait to change the more they feel their soul's crushing weight. So instead many start to inwardly self-defecate to avoid repenting from their mistakes. Repenting is just renewing of the mind, accepting you don't know the way to life. If you did; you'd be happy right? So why suicide? Many would rather die than carry their cross past the finish line.

I STILL WANT TO LIVE

Even if my breaths are linked to death

I still draw life deep into my chest.

How blessed I can watch birds in their nest,

Nuzzling at the breast they remind me without pain; love wouldn't exist.

Beauty hides inside a beautiful soul's eyes,

There are no bad times in a great mind,

Can't find light if your looking for night,

Can't be fire if you don't fight to stay alight.

You may say "why?"

I say "why not?",

This life; is the prize we sought,

Your soul is happy with the chance it got.

So will you or will you not

Make the most with what you've got?

For only then can God guide you to the top,

Only then will you find out why

You had to start at the bottom of the rocks.

WHAT BEAUTIFUL MUSIC

Heavy breathing in my bedroom,

Judging myself like it's a courtroom,

Regrets are framed in my heart's darkroom

While joyful moments are locked in the storeroom.

My anxieties swell into a balloon

"I hope happiness finds me soon",

Doctoring my sorrows at the saloon

In hopes I'll drink myself into somebody new.

Then I hear a familiar tune,

"3 little birds" by Marley

Rocking to the beat; smiling slowly

"The sun does shine doesn't she?"

Suddenly my nightmare was made a dream.

I started thanking God for memories

That helped shape me into a wise oak tree

"God, thank you for reminding me tomorrow doesn't have to be my history"

And in that moment; I found some peace.

DO IT

Even if it's a little cloudy,

Even if the plan is hazy,

Even if it sounds crazy,

Do it; and see why God is amazing.

Everything is changing,

Everyday we're dying,

Everyone is somebody,

Everybody has something.

Live.

Give.

Be;

A gift.

Accept it:

God; is it.

Leave the world,

It hates your magic.

It's up to you what you want out of all this,

To be God's kid or the devil's trick.

I was there and all I can say is this:

The world wants to keep you sick

But God wants to make your life rich.

A DREAM OF DEATH

The grave is a good friend, I think about it a lot, how it'll hug me in darkness under a crystal rock. I think of the sentiment "how sweet, you're padded with pillows just for me". As I dwell on these thoughts I fall into a dream where I've passed on, I see I wasn't a bad a man, an ebony box covered in golden psalms; with families weeping "You were a good man" as everything becomes calm.

I see my daughters and sons, I see my wife waiting for me by the sun for our last dance until we move on, and as bad as I would like to stay "I'm ready to go home today". I meet her in the sky with the cheesiest line "always knew you were my sunshine", she laughs "I love you silly, still the funniest man I know even after our time", I slowly slip her fingers into mine as we slow dance towards the light.

Passing through a watery veil; we find ourselves in the hands of an archangel, I look into her eyes "you really are my angel", she looks at me "you really are my man of fable", tears swell as we're carried to God's table. Now standing at the gates she says to me "I'm sorry, it's time to wake up baby", my voice breaks "why does it have to be this way", she smiles

> *"Because they still need you babe".*

THEY WERE FAKE

I remember that little bus, how happy, all of us was. Giggling at stupid things that today are now joyful memories, so much color is in our history if we choose to see, it wasn't all bad, always a lighthouse in our mind's dark sea. It's okay to say "I miss the old days" as long as you know it's passed away, as long as you know going back would be a mistake.

You miss the blissful ignorance of a "true kiss", you miss the idea that with them you "might have kids", a fantasy you drew in your head, denying the reality they were drawing instead. To them; they were playing house, but to you; this wasn't a dollhouse, you loved them deep down but they just wanted to entertain you like a clown.

Trying to give you something they themselves couldn't find, trying to give you peace of mind. Little did they know that requires work deep inside, so by the time they realized the love you offered was one that climbed; they panicked cause they wanted to stay in the dark all night. Promise me this…

That you'll love yourself first this time.

WHY DO WE LIVE

You got your wish,

You feel nothing but bliss,

How do you feel? Flawless?

Or do you feel its emptiness?

No sorrow means no joy,

Knowing only silence you craved noise.

Creation is a gift disguised as hardship,

Don't you like this? Sailing through life in your emotional starship?

We toil to feel worthy of our tilled soil,

We cultivate ourselves with a shovel labeled:

"Struggle" to express the life we wish to model.

For this is life:

A place where souls mold themselves with a cudgel.

A MOTHER'S LOVE

She held you in her arms, with one thought "what a beautiful star". Seeing you as the best piece of her heart, that's why she calls you her "sweetheart". Inside the womb; she gave the best food, "only the best for you" as she ate your favorite fruits. Cared for your needs before her own, worked her hands to the bone to give you a happy home.

Through tears, pains, and strain, she bought you your favorite games. Raising you best she could, being the parent she wished hers would, loving you in a way that healed her own wounds. So remember, even when you're older, she still wants to be loved like a mother, she still wants you to come over and hug her.

To her your more than just a stranger, you're a part of her soul she held above fire, you're every hope she ever whispered, you're the amber she formed inside her. Never think you're anything less than perfect when she thinks about you; for to her you're an angel she brought life too.

THE LOVE INSIDE OUR PICTURES

I can already see it, laughing over old images with our kids, stories of "the good days" keeping them on their toe-tips, listening close to prevent memory from missing a single strip. Such a beautiful moment, every picture brings a heartfelt mixture, each one pulls a story from our heart's harbor, as we recall memories we're welded further together.

You're so lovely, I'm so lucky, we'll be buried under a redwood tree, joined through the roots; to be as close as we can be. The love inside our pictures will carry our children through storms of their own marital chapters. "How do you do it?" he'll whisper, "we love each other, we compromise instead of wrestle over power", "But it's not that simple father" he'll mutter.

I'll look him in the eyes and reply:

"What if she was no longer alive? Would it matter then who was wrong or right? Is the union all about you? Or is it about a balance of the two? Tell me son: if she was crying alone in the room what would you do? I pray you'd choose to be her king and not some self-centered fool"

TO BE OR NOT TO BE

To be or not to be;

That is the question.

To live a life that's free

Or slave for acceptance.

Your reflection,

Hell or Heaven?

What do you see?

Which direction?

By your judgment;

You invite self-oppression,

By your grace;

You invite self-compassion.

We're all stumbling in a dark place,

We need lights to show the way,

So many cling to lies out of pride,

A choice that breaks so many lives.

What will it be:

Die or Thrive.

Who will you be:

Shadow or Light.

"Be what you want to see",

For this is your time

To hide or shine.

THE OUTCASTS

I choose to be kind, I've been left out all my life. Never, would I want you to feel what I was given, for this is why I give the forgotten so much attention. In them I see an old version, made different to demonstrate how to be authentic, marked at birth to be one of the chosen children, leading a life of rebellion to spite the psychosis of the collective system.

Refusing the default directive; they smile through the hive's hatred, a walking aberration, choosing to be a disruption, radiating the very essence of freedom, a perfect image of how God intended creation. To walk a road made for us alone, to chisel ourselves into who we want to be known, not follow another to find home.

So many try to stop them, out of jealousy for them becoming what they gave up on, for becoming a testimony for the fruits of discipline, shining forth character that is only carved with hardship. Hate them all you want, for while you spend your time trapped in talk; they're always on the hunt.

THE MAN IN THE MIRROR

I know something.

I know; I know nothing.

I know this nothing is a dream,

A play; playing out a cosmic scene.

Where I the puppet choose a role to be,
Where the puppeteer asks
"Are you sure you want this destiny?"
Where I answer "More than anything".

So from the cutting of my old strings
I'm asked to let go of the old things,
To let go of the identity I no longer wish to be
And embrace the new character made for me.

Yet, it stings,
Yet, I weep,
Yet, I scream
For how "it used to be".

Now I can't go back,
Now I'm already here,
Now It's to late,
I've already become;

The Man In The Mirror

TOGETHER THEN

She, my queen,

I, her king.

Numbered with transgressors

We became peaceful aggressors.

Armies spill from the dark one's tower,

On the field, we wait for the coward.

We pray aloud to the heavenly King

Roaring "Greater is He! That is in Me!"

Staring down the enemies forces

We mount our battle-born horses,

Drawing swords of fire we sound the horn,

Legions of angels outpour; ready for war.

As the shadows tremble

From heaven's rumble

We charge forth knowing they'll crumble,

For God is with us,

And they attended their own funeral.

THE FORMULA TO LIFE

        Birth.
        Sin.
        Pleasure.
        PAIN.
        Lost.
        Broken.
        God.
        LOVE.
        Saved.
        Forgiveness.
        Wisdom.
        Repentance.
        Purpose.
        Growth.
        Family.
        Joy.
        Death.
        Life.
        ~
        The Key.

STOP BEING A RAT!!!

Coming out from the black hole

To shove food down your pipe-hole,

Got enough energy to be fiending,

But not enough to be changing?

No wonder we feel guilty,

We've been acting trashy,

As one thinks; so they become,

Want to be a bum? Keep acting like a chump!!!

I say all this out of love,

If I didn't care I'd say

"Do whatever you want"

But I don't want you to wind up a runt.

Go ahead and say I'm "being to blunt",

That's what you'll be if you keep smoking blunts,

Not sharp, not smart, just some incompetent pup.

You say "SHUT UP!", I say "OR WHAT?"

What could you possibly do?

Because right now you're just a weak cub

And nobody wants to be with someone

Who has the will and spirit of a bug…

MOVE!!!

I'm ripping through every demon hiding in my skull!

They sweat pools every time I give the chainsaw a pull,

Been locked up to long, giving them a curb stomp

While grinding their teeth into the wall!

My family needs me to be strong!!!

I won't let them fall for my disobedience to answer my call,

I hear "SHOW THEM ALL! FOR YOU ARE A CHILD OF GOD!

YOU ARE THE HEAD; NOT THE TAIL, MOVE LIKE IT! DO NOT FAIL!!!"

I've put my heart at the end of a flail crushing everything that's a spawn of hell!!!

I see now why they wanted me to stay a clown,

To keep me from retrieving my rightful crown,

They don't like me now that I'm loud, GOOD!!!

IT'S THEIR TURN TO KNOW HOW IT FEELS TO BE

PUT DOWN!!!

I'M NOT DOING ENOUGH

"Just take some rest"

No

"Keep your eyes closed"

I'll rip your throat.

"You've done enough"

You're a joke

"Stop being a grump"

Stop being a chump.

"Why so mean?"

Why so lazy?

"You're an angry baby"

You're just a crybaby.

"Why not take it slow?"

We have, it's why we're still below.

"Remember, peace is important"

REMEMBER TO MUCH OF ANYTHING

IS POISON!!!

I WISHED

This is what I wished for, a mind that mirrors Cat Cheshire, putting all my gold on the alter; my mind was altered, I heard "do not falter" as the answers I sought engulfed my grey matter. Snapping "This is madness!", Realizing "joy is sadness", whispering "I've taken breath for granted", finding "life is a canvas" with colors depending on the artist.

The price for authenticity is being seen as one with insanity, the cost you pay is loss of identity; in exchange for your own brand of sanity, be careful with the dice you're gambling, this covenant with spirit isn't just rambling. Every angel and demon took note, all echoed "here we go" when you opened your heart to the great unknown.

People will label you a clown, even give you a "talking down", but notice they only do so when others are around, with no crowd they feel "I'm no one now", they only stand proud for the recognition of saying what their circus is to scared to say aloud. The pressure of "Becoming" is a dive few survive, yet, that very pressure is the same thing that brings out who you are on the inside.

MAD POET

Me? Mad?

I thought you'd never ask!

I have madness on tap,

Would you like a glass?

No? Then why ask?
The way I see is different from you,
All my answers are subjective to the room,
Everything I know is just a "belief" to you.

Believing is doubting.
Knowing is witnessing.
You cannot know and believe.
One is factual; the other is fractals.

But what is "fact", who could really say?
What if one day; night became day?
Seems the "known" was blown away,
It's the same for what I and others say.

We're all mad, it's just a matter of which madhouse you want to play.

YOU SAID!!!

These memories scream at me, so many women whispering "I love you baby". Seeing only the shadows I wanted to see, even when light exposed their being I still covered them in the shade of my co-dependency. Developed an addiction to the venom in my veins, I didn't feel like me without the "love" they gave, bitten by so many snakes I almost put myself in the grave.

So many times I should've turned the page but every time I saw myself I felt disgrace, so I stayed with the ones who would just tolerate. I truly believed I was a stupid kid with a man's face, always looking for someone else to help me be saved that I lowered my worth to that of a knave; in hopes someone would throw a key in my cage.

The longer I waited; the longer I dismissed how I was treated and the deeper my sorrow buried itself in sadness. Until one day I was thrown into the deep end of madness, It was heaven's way of saving me from the abyss's blackness. I have the heart of a child, so I would've been beaten for awhile if God didn't make me go wild, so even if my past gnaws at me, I remember what He told me:

"You are made new in Me"

LAZY FATHER

Don't want to do it?

Rather spend time wasted?

Treating your growth like an option,

Feeling failure so you don't even clock in.

Want it all done wrapped in a basket

To skip the painful process of progress.

I'm sorry to say, many struggle everyday,

What makes you so special you can't carry your cross's weight?

Nothing, and you feel it.

Many are counting on you to make the right decision,

I know it's hard to be the first not to commit treason.

You think "why wasn't our family enough of a reason?

Why didn't our father pull us out of our icy prison?"

But now you see. You see exactly why he ran from responsibility.

It's torture to realize you're an idiot for the way you live your life and see from your wanting to get high; you lower the chances of your family having a great life.

To change all of who you are doesn't happen overnight, so of course the coward fled into the night, It wasn't in him to be the first sacrifice to bring his family to the light.

So now the pendulum has swung to you,

So I ask you:

What will

YOU

Do?

REALITY?

I don't even know if all this is real, just reflections of myself living in their own reel, being shifted through their own personal levels of reality based on how actions are revealed. How do I know if who I'm speaking to is the actual or the Doppler? How do I know the one that "loves me" isn't just some conjured reward for continuing to serve; and the moment I don't meet the standard is ripped away as punishment for my "nerve", or worse, is torn away for "something higher than what's observed".

In my search for God I've learned why answers are so well locked, I find it's impossible to fight against divine law, if you don't do what is called; you'll be relocated to a different spot, where you'll endure so much pain you'll come back with your head down as you crawl. "Suicide" doesn't save you from life at all, you'll just wake up in bed unable to walk. Yet, in the timeline you left; you're as good as dead and your family must live with the dread.

Whereas in the one you entered; you get to live with the impact of what you did, seeing your family break from the action you decided to commit. Souls think they can escape the curse and gift of life by trying to leave it, you control nothing. You have two choices: work with purpose or suffer consequences of trying to run away from it.

DEVIL'S TRICKS

The devil waves bottles in my face, using loved ones to get me to "take a break", a popping of a cap followed by "take a sip for God's sake". Displaying even in good company I'm not safe, using family to try and crack my character's safe so they wind up getting the wrong side of my rage.

I'm mad at the spirit; not the face, mad at the writer; not the page, mad at the snake; not the cage. It's always the small links that make the chain, little by little, darkness will justify itself with idols, just like angels; devils sow seeds to take root in your temple, same old trick, same old devil.

He'll weaponize the past by tying the anvil around your ankles with a rope weaved from your past articles, he'll put every ounce of who you once were under the scalpel, attempting to keep the plan he has for you actionable, but if he says you're a "devil" and you keep showing you're God's child

Then the charges are dropped for "This one isn't the same criminal"

FEEL THE WHIP

I feel like I'm always going to fail you, I know whipping me with the truth is the best thing to do; but at this point only fear of you is pushing me through. If I wasn't afraid of your wrath I'd already coated the wall behind me in a bloodbath, at the same time I can't go back, trying to reload old chapters will just make me go mad.

I learned from what I've had, I know sadness is a trap but what do you do when the lies become facts. "It is what it is" isn't enough to make sense of this, this war between being a slave with purpose and being a fool with happiness; is stretching my spirit thin.

The irony of wanting this then hating it; is as ironic as thinking kids bring fulfillment. It's funny because I'd rather live with knowing the truth than die living a lie, I guess what I'm doing is grieving the lack of responsibility I had in the old times, It was fun I can't lie but truth be told… I rather God lash me; than demons feed on my light.

KILL THE DEMONS

WHAT IF YOUR CHID SCREAMS

FROM THE HALLWAYS OF THEIR BAD DREAMS

FOR DADDY TO HELP CHANGE WHAT THEY SEE!?!

COULD YOU!!! OR ARE YOU JUST DEMON FEED?

YOU STAND FOR NOTHING THEN YOU ARE NOTHING!

SAY SOMETHING!!! YOU SAID YOU WOULD DO ANYTHING!!!

THEN FIGHT THE DOUBT, RAGE AGAINST THESE CLOWNS!!!

THE DEVIL WANTS YOU DOWN TO TAKE YOUR FAMILY DOWN!!!

WAKE UP!!! WAKE UP!!! WAKE UP!!!

STAND UP!!! STAND UP!!! STAND UP!!!

UNLESS YOU'RE OKAY WITH DEMONS DEFILING YOUR OWN FLESH AND BLOOD!!!

G E T U P !!!!

PLEASE FATHER... FORGIVE ME...

I've never had a real Father, so please forgive me for my emotional squalor, I've survived by crying from the heart, many take pity and just leave me in the dark. I'm not used to falling apart in someone's arms, I'm not used to someone trying to fix my broken parts, I'm not used to having my tar washed away by a pure heart.

It's scary thinking "they might actually love me", every time I love somebody they just use me, but this is different, because I have nothing yet you've given me everything, trusting I'll become something; from the seeds you've sown me.

I'm still learning to cope without the devil's dope, thank you for filling my soul with hope when I feel broke, thank you for saving me from the rope, thank you Father for revealing life away from you is a joke, that any other path is clouded in smoke.

I love you Dad, please forgive my arrogance when I'm mad.

THE ROSE IN MY HEART

Nobody knows about my rose, or how or why it grows, let me tell you how I know. Pain is everywhere, and everyone is hurting, when I see blood I come running. They look at me "why help this nobody?", pressing on their chest; pain swelling "they are us, why aren't you helping?", they laugh as if I'm joking

"They're broken for a reason, they'll drain you and leave, we don't understand why you care for this cretin". Still my hands slam their chest centerline trying to revive the heart inside, pure rage erupts from my eyes "THIS IS A LIFE!!! HOW CAN YOU WATCH THEM DIE!!!", the devils laugh almost to a cry

"They chose this, they could repent, but instead wallow in sin". As the light in them dims I reach within and grab my rose's stem "I know your pain, you were abandoned", carefully I stitch what's broken "you are not what has happened", pulling them close I say "you are the magic that makes light from madness" suddenly he breathes and squeezes close to me

"Thank you for not leaving me in that darkness"

CAN'T SAY

Can't say I didn't stand my ground, blood still on the walls where I was found, in the back of my head just below my crown. Standing on the edge of destruction I made a decision, that I would continue my construction no matter the situation. Choosing to add value with actions that say "I'll climb out of this well", can't lie sometimes I fell, met by the black waters of my own personal hell.

But I always start again, determined to escape death, I refuse to be a captive of flesh, everyday I claw my way up like I'm in the final stretch, because tomorrow I might wind up dead and my final moments will be me fighting the demons in my head. I lead a life I would want for my kids, so excuse me if you're offended I don't slip.

If I do, believe it won't happen again, I've lived in my sin and let me tell you it's better to repent, it's just a changing of lens, it's understanding the way you live is a dead end, it's accepting you've been running away from who you really are within, recognize what you've been given, there's a piece of God inside you waiting to be opened.

GHOST CAT

On the streets of souls I walk the fence line watching life unfold, I see many lives through different windows, a mom yelling at her 14 year old while another wishes her's would come home, a son waiting for his father to show while another takes for granted his own, parents burying the same children they said were "so annoying, you don't even know!".

I've seen pain, I've seen grace, I've even seen both in the same place, have you ever seen true forgiveness take place? For a moment, you can feel the reason for releasing someone from a great weight, you can see how regret stains their face, like how a child makes a grave mistake, you find through their shame how we're all the same.

I wish they'd love each other more, I wish they'd open more doors, I wish I wasn't just a cat witnessing suffering in the world. If I was ever alive again I'd remember "they're only human" and by my choosing to let go; I free myself from pain I don't have to hold. Also, just so you know, before I died, a wise man looked at me and said

"We're just pieces of a grander whole."

"IF" I REACH THE GATES

When I die and stand in front of you; there's only one thing I can do, "please, don't send me away from you". I know I was never enough, I should've done more then what was done, I'm sorry I was never your perfect son, I know self-pity won't save me from what you judge, but I did love, I did pour out my whole cup for those in the mud, I know I've messed my life up; but please Father, don't leave me in lockup.

Never thought I'd relate to Judas, or why he ended it, couldn't live knowing he condemned the only one who cared about him, is this why I hide in sin? So I don't have to sit with the shame of what I did? I already hate myself for not letting you save me for as long as I did because by saying I love you and being half-in; I condemned your character by not being all in. I'm supposed to be the result of what you can do and if I'm not listening then that looks bad on you.

It's not just about me, now I see, by you healing me I become a stream that others can follow back to the beginning because in the end it's always the same thing: it all leads back to you. The all-loving God who holds the universe from splitting in two, I now see why and what I have to do, please God, just let me wake up in my room and everyday forward I'll just worship you.

A PUPPET NAMED STITCH

There once was a puppet named stitch.

Made from the maker's favorite tree,

Crafted his heart from the watch in his pocket,

Molded his mind into a heart shaped locket.

He said "your life will be a hard one,

You'll let so many give your strings a tug,

But from being drug through the mud;

You'll teach others self-love"

Oh, and he did feel it,

The "I LOVE YOU'S" and "YOU ARE ME'S"

Were really just about getting him to sacrifice his own needs.

Fell in love with the wrong one; and didn't want to leave,

Found out after chapter one; some just aren't meant to be.

Found out most puppets don't mean what they say,

That most are just looking to dance their life away,

"It's a shame" he would say, "I wish they'd love me the same way".

But he wasn't perfect and he knew it too,

No matter the partner, he'd screw it up too,

Like if they brought fire then he did too,

Learning "I still have my own issues".

That day he began what he was created to do,

Making antidotes from the pain he consumed

The Maker smiled and said "You've entered book two,

And every chapter is named the same thing:

Learn How to Love You"

KNOCK, KNOCK

BOOM, BOOM, Gos the double barrel thunder-cannon!

BANG, BANG, Go the soldiers tricked by mammon!

KNOCK, KNOCK, Go the devils demanding children!

YES, YES, Answers the investors profiting destruction!

They'll send yours but "NOT MINE!"

There would be no war if they had to send their bloodline.

Everyone knows it's hell disguised as "doing what's right",

Maybe not then, but definitely now, wars today are for resources and power.

God bless the troops that fought against tyrants,

Thank God for the soldiers that protect our nation,

I just don't think it's right those that signed can hide, "crazy conversation"

If you're authorizing the taking of life then you should be on the frontline, no hesitation.

I have a problem the same hands that sign also war-profiteer

But then again everyone hears what they want to hear.

And nobody cares until they lose somebody dear,

Only when our children die will we see the bigger picture.

GO!

Gotta go! Gotta go! Never does anything slow!

Always burns out after pulling the whole load,

Does everything in aggressive spurts, sound like someone you know?

I hope so, because I'm hear to remind you there's always going to be another goal.

If you can't be happy in the process, you won't be when you finally get access.

Obsessing about an over-romanticized moment when you can "finally have it!"

Soon to find it doesn't mean as much as you thought it did;

Wishing you could go back and say "don't do what I did!"

You find out the hard way society wants what's good for them,

And that your pursuit of happiness was all just comedy to them,

And by the time you reach your deathbed it's to late to "start again",

At that moment you'll realize it was always about you and not them

That it was actually your life; you were supposed to be living in.

THE ARTIST WITHIN

I've never been normal; I've always seen the magic in the abnormal. Where most would see a blackhole I see a hole yearning to be whole. I can't help it; how I'm designed, being an artist is over-romanticized. Everyone thinks it's "so fun" to be everyone's favorite art spun; but don't want the inspiration from where it comes from.

It requires a mountain of pain to gather the clay for what artists make, the fires we survive put our minds at stake, some hurt so deeply that its our own lives we take, we create from a place where the air is heavy with heartbreak, where everything that's truly beautiful comes from what breaks.

Many don't know; only a few do, the amount of suffering we plow through to get the art to you. We're alone, we're walking ghosts, we're one bad day away from "going home". We see death differently, we see peace but know that "answer" is a disease, life is a gift we know, it's just for us, it really hurts to grow.

I'M SORRY

I got blood on you; I'm sorry, you felt my heart bleed but didn't even cut me, I've been abandoned so many times I expect you to run, my heart is scarred from those I used to love. Forgive the broken boy inside me, he doesn't believe you could love him really, always counting his mistakes but never gives himself grace, giving his heart away because he believes his chest isn't a safe place.

Please wait for me, I'm still learning to breathe after drowning in a dark sea. Sometimes I split; I see things in black and white, I'm still learning to control this damaged mind, I now see how it created a cracked lens to protect me from anymore "lies". Please give me patience, I'm working to correct it, I really want to be fixed; please don't leave me in this ditch.

That's always happened before, that's why I keep thinking and preparing for you to close the door, it's how I've protected myself before, but I see how that can sabotage what we're trying to work towards. I want you more than you could ever know, please don't ever think I actually "want to be alone".

A DAY TO REMEMBER

What a day, a day where I got exactly what I prayed, a day where it felt I held you for days. Yes, we had a few drinks; and yes we did all the sexy things but nothing compares to the way you made my heart sing, never in my life have I ever wanted so bad to get a wedding ring, while we were out I saw a glimpse of your wings.

Angel in disguise; you're not fooling me, the eyes don't lie; there's a piece of heaven I see. And oh my; how they bring me to my knees. Trapped in thought across the table as we eat "why on earth is she with someone like me?", I think we think alike, I think you see me the way I see you and that's why; you're mine.

After we ate we watched our favorite show, the best part to me was when I got to hold you close, listening to your breaths makes my heart slow, you're my peace in the chaos we all know, and you mean so much to me I hope you know; that you're a part of me I call home.

LETTING MYSELF GO

I can't hold onto you, the cracked parts that split me in two, an identity that craves acceptance from fools. Accepting words from the past that cut our value in half; letting others treat us like broken glass; how can we find love in this eyeless mask? how can we stand if we keep letting demons pull us below sands at the slightest glance of being a real man.

We only have one life and you know it too, the old has to die in order to be made new, I'm not leaving you; I'm carrying you, I'm looking at everything you've been through with a different view, I can't keep trying to march in your ripped up shoes, we'll both die with regret if I don't do what's best for you, I love you; I'm choosing to get in front of you.

You're just a child, you don't know any better, I'll lead us to better weather, I'm going to be the father we never had, aren't you happy? To finally have a dad? Please don't be mad, there's still so many good memories to be had, so many gifts I have for you to be unwrapped, to do things for you that will heal what makes you so sad.

You think them leaving us proves you're bad, but I won't leave you, I'm proud to say you're apart of my past.

BROKEN LOVER

When others love they pour from the top of their cup, leaving some inside to stay wholesome, a way of saying "I'm also worth loving". But mine has hole at the bottom where I see my lover as the answer to my problems, where I gain my value from how I'm viewed, where when I break; I make them the glue, which splits who I am in two, caught in between what I want and "I'd do anything for you".

All the attention, all the care, all the things one needs to "make it there" I'd give to them without a care, for how they make me feel matters more than what I'm working towards, so anytime their behavior switched; it ripped at my heart's chords triggering memories of past horror when a devil took full advantage of my natural core, causing me to spiral to protect against pain that once went viral.

Sealing off the hole I go cold and remove myself from the other's hold, for "I know" they're planning to leave me in the snow after they get bored of "the same old show". I'm see through, I wear my heart on my sleeve and wear it proud too, I'd give up everything for the ones I love, I know this because it's something I've already done, where I split open my cup to save them from mistakes they've done.

Still, I was abandoned by all of them, so of course I'm a lover with a broken cup, forever looking for the one who sees I'm just as worthy to be filled up.

SAD CAT

Once there was a cat who was different from the whole litter, he didn't have the most desirable features, a black cat with eyes of yellow; he was called "bad luck's shadow", his brothers and sisters all found a home; but for him people judged him by his coat, "he's evil" they would gloat, so as months turned into years he began to feel shame for what others sneered.

Until a woman so kind came "how much for the cat? I want to buy". For the first time he felt alive, more so when he was brought home, brushed everyday and told "you have the best coat I hope you know", everything was exactly what he hoped. But one day something in her changed, one day with a devilish grin she said "come here Mr. Shadow, I want to play a game".

He saw a blade in her hand and a wooden mannequin of him on the table stand, he ran under the bed but was grabbed by the scruff of his neck, suddenly he was slammed on the kitchens cutting board and as she raised the knife above her head with all the strength he had left he broke free and clawed her eyes bloody red, screaming she ran to her door to ask her neighbors for help.

As she opened the door he bolted outdoors, running as fast as he could into the woods, he found a cave to hide in; as he should, and as a tear dropped from his eye; he thought "I really thought someone actually cared about me this time".

THEY ALL LIE TO ME!!!

Everyone that's close always ends up cutting my soul, of course I feel cold, of course depression has me in a chokehold, of course my heart is riddled with holes. Why do I continue to love these people who just leave me the minute there's nothing left to squeeze? Why do I actually believe they'll stand by me? Why am I so naive all the time?

Am I really so lonely I'll gladly swallow lies? Is my reflection so broken that everyone else seems perfect in my eyes? I guess I'm just an ignorant child, I guess I'll always be the one that's mocked and exiled, I guess I'll always be an easy mark for those looking to defile. Always unloved, always a useless pile.

Everyone thinking "he's so dramatic" until I switch the safety to automatic; and blow my cares away from their godless antics. Most pretend to love God to trick the flock into praising their version of "God's grace"; and show "the right way" to get into heaven's gates, hypocrites galore seems to be the human race.

I hate how humanity loves to hate and indulge in the fake, and yes you guessed it, that means

IT'S MYSELF I HATE!!!

WORK!!!

You lazy bastard, children around the world with an empty cupboard; yet here we are eating and being "bored", shooting shots at anyone who says "hey there" acting like a whore. Got all the time to slave after "a good time" but not enough to change your life. You smell like desperation, you feel like everything wrong with the nation.

Are you proud of yourself? Wasting all your potential? Proving what everyone says not to be false? Letting them control your thoughts, letting them take away what makes you special; because deep down you never really wanted it at all. For if they're right you don't have to fight, what an excuse to keep living in lies.

This journey isn't all light, it REQUIRES you to burn away what is keeping you away from your desired life. God isn't dumb, He won't reward a bum, or someone who thinks and acts like a chump, that looks bad on Him and won't cater to sin. So if your content being away from Him; go ahead, take that sip.

I CAN'T RUN AWAY

This is who I am, all these letters and all these words they're apart of my soul, I can't control how my mind wants to explore every creative fold, I'm letting go. Getting wonderfully lost in the only gift I've got, I smile at the page and thought "you're the only one who understands my thoughts". I used to hate the way my mind would race but now it's not so bad when I keep the pace.

I'm not doing this for fame, I'm not doing this for a name, I'm doing this to help somebody's life change from how I'm healing my pain. After my first poem I was never the same, I was amazed, the way my whole view of the world changed. Everything became poetic, I became fluent in art's dialect, every time my soul had an idea I'd answer collect, and my hysteria became the source of silk in my web.

I'm so happy I didn't stay in the boxes others tried keep me, it took a lot of trying to be "everybody's something" to realize what they really wanted was for me to stay nothing. "Misery loves company" is absolutely true, always pulling you down the minute you start becoming you. They love you in the beginning for chasing your dreams; but hate you later for reminding them you have to try again to succeed.

MY CHERRY BEE

I know what you're going to say sweetie "you're so cheesy". I can't help I'm the queso to your nachos or how I pair so well to the fine wine of your soul, you say I'm cold well you're definitely fire, melting down my walls with your wildfire, helping me learn to love again with my heart still riddled in shellfire, taking time to help me rewire when I go haywire, I caught feelings for you quicker than an umpire.

You're the best part of my day, you're one of best parts when I pray, your words to me are like rays from the sun; shining on parts of me that've been dying for so long, you're the cherry bee I've been waiting for my lifelong, I'll talk to you all nightlong till we find what's wrong, digging until we find the bedrock of the problem that slams against your walls.

I know you've always been strong, I know you're everyone's rock, but I'm the key to your lock and you're the battery in my clock, and together our dreams we'll unlock. I hope this poem made you happy or smile at least; because I always do when I think about you and me. I love you baby, you're all the puzzle pieces I need.

THIS IS ME TAKING A BREAK

This is my video game, this is the dopamine I crave, this is the dream I chase. And in case you don't believe, I still wish you the best in creating what you want to see, I'm to happy to let others opinions weigh on me, I want you to find your something so you can feel how I'm feeling, just letting go and trying to be the best at who you choose to be.

I don't know why so many want to see others in agony, maybe because they feel that way about themselves? It's a mystery, but one thing I do know is if I keep passing out honey I'll attract bees that'll help pollinate the other flowers around me. I love you; I hope you know you're everything you ever needed to glow.

Sure there's pain but without it we would never know true fulfillment for our happy face, you'd be amazed at what you can do. Realize living your dream was always the path God wanted you to take, and how you're more than qualified to take up space, you've been more than worthy to release yourself from your own cage. We'll do it together, come on, let's turn the page.

A BUNNY IN A CASTLE

One day a bun-bun with flippity-floppities hopped into a castle to explore the great mystery, with big hippity-hoppities he eventually found out it was empty, "so this is all for me?" He said gleefully. He jumped from tables and swung from the chandeliers ceiling; abounding in joy he shouted "EVERYTHING HERE IS AMAZING!!!"

He ran back to tell the other rabbits but soon found they weren't having it "you shouldn't be there, you're just a rabbit". To which he smiled and got wide eyed "nobody's there, it can be our home away from night, besides, it's a far better shelter", they all laughed "we have everything we could ask for, we're fine out here,"

He frowned "what if a storm passes through here?", the colony became mad "IF YOU LIKE IT SO MUCH THEN GO BACK!!!", and he did, and as crazy as it sounds a storm did pass through and destroyed everything the others clung too, yet he still was sad for the family he used have "I was just trying help them live a better path".

THE UNREADABLE BOOK

In a library so vast, books congregate to talk about how many people read their pages in the past as a way to prove the value they have, "I've had 8" one boasted from the back, "I've had 19" one laughed. As they all went around they eventually came to the last in the crowd, "LOOK" a dark book yelled like a siren, "IT'S THE UNREADABLE ONE" he shouted.

Covered in dots he walked away as they mocked. "Why does no one ever want read what I have in stock" beating himself up with self-talk "Nobody wants to be caught with a book with spots" he weeped while back and forth he rocked "I'll always be the laughingstock, the best I can do is just pray someone will want to interlock"

So he prayed "please God send someone my way", he didn't know if it would work but had no other options and was hurt. The very next day a woman came in with a cane and asked for him by name, the bookkeeper grabbed him and said "this is one I've never seen touched until today", she smiled "I like it that way".

She put him on the table and put her fingers to the braille on the paper, the others were shocked "no one has ever felt us like that before". From her face came tears, she went to the front and said "I'll take this one, I have the money for it, here", the old man smiled "well now, looks like our loneliest book has a girlfriend now", she laughed "yeah, I love it now"

Once all was paid and done he asked "by the way, what page made you cry like a little one?", to which she replied "John 3:16:

> *For God so loved the world, that he gave his only begotten son, that whoever believes in him shall not perish, but have eternal life.*

That one."

THE MONSTER BELOW THE SURFACE

Twitching… Everywhere… itchy… What did they say to me?

Who's this shadow testing me? This empty husk of meat.

They poke… They prod… Pick-locking what I keep locked,

The hammer is almost cocked, why do they want to rot?

Could've just left us alone but instead chose today to go "home".

Blood is running cold, speaking bold but haven't made a move

So you must've saw the ghost deep below the surface of my soul,

The part that's angry and hollow, the part that hates the world for being shallow.

Everything around me will be used to send you to the gallows.

I've never fought fair, can you feel it in my stare? I. Don't. Care.

"Me or you" was always an easy choice to choose, I. Won't. Lose.

Walk away while you still have your back and neck in place;

Or feel my rage as they break.

THE VOICES IN MY HEAD

Scratching; never lacking in the punches they're packing, things I thought I left in passing become ammo for harassment; laughing that I belong in a casket. If I didn't know any better I'd think they're trying to stop me from reaching the place God tasked me; and being demons of course they want me in darkness chained to blackness

"Never belonged there, always been a liar, just a son of fire". I smile knowing I was called by my Father, refusing to drown in the same water I used to squalor I let go of all the limits I used to harbor so I can reach the life I desire, walking through the fire shielded by my savior, devils in my way? "Time to meet your maker".

"Come on, just one drink" trying to get me to sink, trying to put me back in chain links, rebuking demons before they sink their teeth, no room for error or the table I'll never reach, no more time leeches; time to listen to what I'm preaching, now the student is the teacher, behold:

The Sinner Has Become The Preacher.

YOU SAY YOU'RE LEAVING

You say you're doing school, you could do it here if you choose. But your heart is a star that yearns to be away from the moon, you know how close I am to you, I say "just make sure to call me, alright?" to which you reply "my education is first, I'll do what I can alright".

My body remembers the pattern, my mind is forecasting disaster, I'm trying to push down the monster; but your actions keep saying you you want to be a runner. I'll always be here for you, but deep down I don't know if when you say "I love you" if it's actually true.

I'll be your partner, but until I know what you choose I can't be your lover. I've been a soldier; I've seen what's happened to my brothers while they were over. Broken hearts and silent screams; as the woman of their dreams ripped their heart out at the seams.

I won't be used just to be discarded because you can't get with me conveniently, I have to protect myself from the possibility of you becoming heartless the moment distance is put between you and me.

A MAN'S DREAM

When I first met you; I never expected the depth of love I'd have for you, the way you lit up the room set my heart abloom, how did you do that? Bring brief peace to the chaos inside my darkroom, it must be for the same reason we're together for the rest of our seasons, you're the piece of me I've been missing.

I know the wedding and the guests, the honeymoon and the rest, but through all of it you're the part that's best. I love how we hold God at the head, I love how we pray every night before bed, I love that you understand without him we never would've met, you're the only world where I want my sun to set.

Are you ready for this foxtrot? The spins, the dips, the way you bend and I lift; because to dance until death with you is a gift and I want to know if you're ready for this. So if you are; we'll seal it with a kiss, it's my favorite part I would never miss, the part where we both say "I do" and begin painting our canvas.

"Wait... Who's this?"

ALWAYS THE WILD ONE

Oooooo it always feels good, the way mind can go from level to daredevil from just being bored in a world of rules, I always felt the same way in school when teachers would look miserable too. I thought "if following the system is so cool then why do they act like ghouls?" And from that day I let it all out, all the crazy they tried to push down.

I became the class clown, not that funny but I didn't care anyhow. Some smiled, some laughed, but every day I felt like a firecracker having a blast. Sure, I could've paid attention, sure I could've went to college, but it just wasn't in me to "SIT DOWN OR IT'S DETENTION!!!", they wanted me submissive and to "listen!!!"

And I tried for a couple seasons but at the end I was just a tad bit to active to be "effective", I was to much of a free soul to let my personality to be collected, oh and how they hated it. The way I wouldn't conform the way they did, I saw firsthand where their actions led.

A life where most of the time they felt dead.

MADNESS

I feel it coming now, everything in my head has gotten loud, I've never fit into a crowd, all by myself is how I live now. Away from everyone who thinks I'm a clown. We'll see who's laughing when I get my crown, I don't need to point and get loud, my actions alone will be enough to put them down, how I handle business will be enough to show "I'm home now".

I love being a "freak", love how from my madness my creativity peaks, everything about me I crafted from the threads of my dreams, "The Madman of Poetry" is what it seems; as I craft rhymes from the ether of my memories, being a conduit for the unseen I've been taught things you wouldn't believe, achieving heights of thought that would drive a normal person to insanity.

It's weird how only the indoctrinated can diagnose "psychosis", how only they can determine if someone is insane, how they can take everything away because "you lost touch with reality so what we're doing is for your own safety, okay?". Isn't it scary? How easy these devils can take things away? Oh well, it's not the first time I've presented an idea and been labeled a nutcase.

JACK IN THE BOX

The way I create is complex, many are perplexed how I can write in ways that seem like a hex. Like Lecter or the Collector when I map lines out for the slaughter, coating each word in laughter because when it comes to poetry I'm The Joker. Painting verbal pictures by spraying pain on the frame with a super soaker named "Life Is A Joke Sir".

Popping out the box like jack with verses that are conjured from abyss's black; to show "he really is the only one who can do magic like that". Wizard with a pen and paper, every letter made with ice and fire, how else could I be "cold" without being a pyromancer? Bringing the dead alive with poems fitting a necromancer; of course I'm a best seller.

In the court of art I'm the jester, dancing on a canvas like the hatter with a grin of Cheshire. Every step a genius stroke from one of the best, quizzing me when I made the test; are you crazy? Wait… YES, I love it when others talk mess, mop it up; squeeze it out into the inkwell on my desk, because as you know "a hater's venom sticks to my paper the best".

THE DEMON IN ME

I remember when I was possessed roaming the streets, dancing with spirits that recognized the jezebel in me, drinking bottles; letting my passions burn on full throttle, getting so high I was practically astral, switching between Hyde and Jekyll; as I drank myself almost clinical, laughing with the others squandering our potential as we reveled in our carnal carnival.

Catching glimpses of myself in the mirror; I saw the smile and teeth of some creature, it didn't matter; I still indulged in the monster's nature. Leading me so far away from the man I am today, just goes to show we all need a history from which we can run away, you learn through the decay that "this life is not okay", you begin seeing how much you're beginning to change.

The moment you try to escape that's when you feel the chains, then you wish you never stepped into that place, the minute you see the devil in your own face is when you call out for grace. That's when you beg to be saved, when you

know in your heart you can't get away in your own strength,
so before you go out tonight to play; I have to say

"Remember there's always a price to pay"

WHY POETRY?

I've been alive since life begun.

I find poetic verse to be quite fun.

A tango between heart and mind;

My mysteries hide in every line.

You may say "Death wouldn't rhyme"

Yet, life and I dance like this all the time.

This is why rhymes are easy to remember,

Poetry mirrors the natural order.

Can't have one without the other

For hot and cold make the temperature.

Truth is found in its literary structure

Showing everything in life has a pattern.

Love and anger, happy and somber,

Hornets and bees, flytraps and trees,

War and peace, pain and release.

A poetic rhythm, like the words on this sheet.

In this book I've written for you;

You'll find secrets all the way through.

So don't leave, or I'll be coming for you…

I knew you'd smile, cause you already knew;

I chase no one, for time pulls me to you.

THEY WERE JUST MEAT

Various souls are claimed by monsters with a human face.

Curious, I peered into each of their minds with my ethereal gaze.

I found most saw a parent who treated them the same way,

Some believed they'd be protected by the monster they praised.

The longer they stayed, the more their essence was stripped away.

But some liked it that way, why else would they accept to be prey?

I've seen mothers treated like slaves leave with children the same day,

Many came from worse and still crafted heaven out of the devil's clay.

The truth is stranger than fiction, I know the carnal fantasies of a human.

I pass no judgement, I merely observe until it's time for collection.

Almost every single one weeps for all the time they've wasted,

Only when I'm close do they give their life much needed reflection.

There are few who have shook hands with me, most ask:

"Why am I treated so badly? Why don't I get the love I give freely?"

I say: "You don't love yourself, you allow dogs to treat you like hell"

They scream "THEY WERE MY FAMILY!!! WHY WOULD'NT THEY JUST SEE!?!"

I say :"I can't help you if you don't take responsibility"

MY ONLY WISH BY: DEATH

I can't remember last I wished,

For I know mine can't be granted.

Yet, I'll share it, it's still poetic.

Listen. It's simple but intricate.

I wish you knew life is a gift.

That your soul craved all this.

Your essence craved experience,

To feel emotions instead of just "happiness".

What other reason is there for creation?

A piece of the creator you have been given,

To make the imagination a manifestation,

From infinite to limited; is why you chose to live.

From everything to nothing

To become everything from nothing.

A dance between the created duality

To choose what role you wish to be.

Hero or villain, slave or civilian,

Opposing elements gives life heartiness.

Without me; breath loses its significance.

Without an end; purpose loses importance.

Did you know the present Is a present?

Yet, once life is opened it's less evident.

It has to be, it's the whole point for being,

In order to receive the highest trophy

Something you were already born with;

Yet still worth grabbing,

A feeling called:

Worthy

I CRIED

I cried once; for a young man that loved,

He gave his heart and was treated like mud,

Gave his all to those with a draining touch,

But He didn't care they were using his love.

He walked around lifting everyone up,

Held children like they were his own blood,

I always saw Him pouring from His cup,

But for Him, the smiles and tears He received was enough.

He only spoke to heal the broke,

Walking around in a dirty cloak,

Yet, His words brought a lump to your throat,

It was like watching a man become hope.

You could've been ready to hang from a rope

And He could resurrect the life in your bones.

Never in all my years have I ever seen a love so fierce,

Those that met Him thought they met God's mirror.

Then I saw it, I saw the nails pierce,

I saw evil men condemn their savior,

Wanting control, they stripped His flesh to the bone,

Wanting to make their point known; they made a cross His home.

As He cried I gripped my scythe ready to take humanity's life,

I waited for our God on high to say "Go, save my Son's life"

Instead I heard "FORGIVE THEM" echo throughout time.

This was it, the one and only time; I Death, have ever

Cried…

MY LOVE STORY

Death in love?

Of course I was,

Only ever once,

Fell for an angel of love.

One that I handed souls to by touch,

She always smiled at me despite my husk.

Didn't think of it much "just courtesy from above"

Yet, one moment at dusk; she cooed these words like a dove:

"You're just as important as the rest of us, thank you love"

This was the first compliment I'd heard in a millennia.

Shaking, I asked her one thing "can I give you a hug?"

She said "of course love"

She came close, I lost my repose, I opened my arms slow,

As I embraced her heavenly glow, for a moment I felt home.

Lost in a feeling I've never felt before; I heard her whisper:

"Don't feel bad, what happens next is a work of the lord"

I then felt her life start to wane toward heaven's door,

As she began to fall to the floor I cried "WHY LORD!!!"

She murmured "pull me closer; feel the love of our Father"

"How is this love?" I whispered in anger, tears falling she said

"Wasn't the moment we shared worth this painful despair?

You deserved to feel real love; even if it was only once,

Don't say it isn't fair, be happy you got to hold me here,

In moments I'll be above, weep for joy, for in God; we are all one"

Grieving, I squeezed her gently "thank you for loving me"

She wrapped her arms around me "this isn't the end lovely",

"What do you mean?", she giggled "I'm an angel remember;

I'll see you tomorrow silly"

HATE

No poison is deadlier than hate,

One drink seals a generation's fate.

Trapped in a tear-filled lake of pain

For the sins of fathers who treated life like a game.

For the want of temporary power;

They killed others for their tower.

The highest form of irony I've ever heard

Was after a kill they called them the "coward".

The inability to attain the outcome desired

Without violence is the true mark of a coward.

An action lead by fear just to not appear as a deer,

Yet, like Rome, a kingdom falls that's built on murder.

I always wonder how long humanity will fight its mirror,

Or how long they'll let the devil continue to be their thinker.

They don't seem to mind as long as they can still be drinkers,

Yet, they cry later about how everything is run by dictators.

I've seen this cycle to many times before,

The less they care about one another

The more they suffer,

But "what do I know"

I'm just a collector.

WHY NOT LOVE?

First, what is Love?

Just know it comes from God,

You ask: "how do we know this?"

Look around, how else do you explain all this?

Everything He is was given to create this experience,

All of it is held together by power beyond comprehension.

He could do anything, but decided to give you moments,

Gave you autonomy to make the decision to love or hate him freely.

All the while loving you no matter what you do,

For you have a piece of Him that is forever inside you.

The hell you put yourself through is because of choices you choose,

"Eternal punishment" is thinking true joy can come without the other half of you.

You were made from the essence of love,

So you'll only find peace by becoming one.

Only by sharing the gift He gave you

Will you find out why love is The Truth.

Yet, you can still "just do you"

But I have only one question:

"Exactly, how is that working

Out for you?"

THE HALLWAYS OF MY MIND

Could anyone really understand? Would anyone care if they knew me like the back of their hand? Why do I care if anyone would love me after knowing my past? Maybe I just want somebody to hold me in their hands and say "I'm so proud you made it through that". Maybe I'm looking for the validation from a dad I never had, maybe for others I break my back just so I can hear "Great job!!! Only you can do that!!!".

Something I've never heard because my real father flew away with the birds. From me feeling like a waste; do I think my only purpose is to help others get their happy face? Did me not having a real dad really affect me that bad? Where I don't feel worthy of having what I want to have? There's a part of me that screams in the back "if we were really all that don't you think he would've stayed where we were at?"

I walk through the hallways of my mind finding pictures in frames that scream "LIES!!!", I try to look for some kind of pride in my old life; but all I see is a broken child trying to prove he's worth the find. Still breaking himself to fit into an image so others will accept him; hurting himself because he believes nobody can love him. But that isn't true, I do love him, and that's why

I'm going to take care of him.

I CAN DO THIS

I can do this, I can finish this book, only I know about all the pain it took, can't fail now my family's life is on the hook. The doubts don't matter any longer, I'll write these words through the fire, I won't abandon my dreams now, I'm so close I'll find the power somehow, set ablaze what's left of my firepower, push myself to the limit because I refuse to be a coward.

My heart's firing on all cylinders, spitting words to paper like a sidewinder; running hard through the crossfire because my soul is made from a tiger. Going higher under heavy shellfire; firing at demons trying to pin me in gunfire, angels providing air support with spitfires as I rage through the wildfires, cutting my way through the barbwires "I will reach my desires!"

I may have blown a gasket, nothing God can't fix, I must finish what I'm tasked with, in so much pain I can no longer mask it. Seeing double vision I slice through enemy lines like an axman, I won't stop, look in my eyes; I'm already a deadman, low on ammo I weaponize the broken bones in my hands, I already told myself "death before dishonor" I'll fight to the end like a madman.

THIS IS WHO I AM

I can't fight it any longer, I'm supposed to forge art in the fires of my heart, I looked in mirror at all the marks only I can see in the dark and said "someone needs the story from my scars". This is the cross I bear, this isn't fun; it's just what I'm called to do here. Sometimes I don't want to reopen the wounds I've seared but I won't let feelings interfere with the healing that comes from me speaking on my pain from past years.

It's my responsibility to take accountability for my abilities and to push myself in ways others wish they could daily, I know others may hate what I embody but that's only because they know they should be doing the same thing. They know they should be growing, they know they should be working, they know everything else is slowly turning them into nothing, I've been there so they can't tell me anything, mostly everybody just wants to be lazy.

It's hard for a reason, the character you cultivate through actions is worth every tearful season. Like the breaking of bones you heal back stronger than before, the reason you're always bored; is because you're not pursuing growth anymore. Don't look at me that way and say "I don't know what I want to do" because at the end of the day you and I both know that's just an excuse not to do the work necessary to become the person God made.

Truth.

WHO AM I?

So you may not know what to do, you may see yourself and ask "who?", but let me ask; what did you used to love to do before the world threw its judgements on you? And before you disown what used to make you glow by saying "I was just a child I didn't know" ask yourself if you're hiding from that passion because somebody else said "it's not as good as their's though". Are you rejecting a part of you to protect yourself from the pain of trying?

For if you fail; you might feel that proves everything of what others were saying, that you're just a failure or a nobody. The broken say these things so you don't remember you're a somebody, they put you down for fear you'll finally escape the illusion they're casting, you really can do anything if you keep trying. They don't want you to grow beyond the image of you they painted because that'll prove they were actually the idiot.

The world treated me the same way when I started writing poems from the very first day. Projecting their own limiting beliefs onto me in hopes I'd give up on my dreams. Hoping I'd become like them: a shell of the potential locked away inside them. Hoping I'd collapse under the weight of their opinions; but I didn't, I saw my gift and I cultivated it, I saw who I really was and went after him, I refused to become the world's art project, I decided to become who I really am and I don't regret it.

I love you, please just… Go for it.

REAPER OF RHYMES

This is my time; couldn't stop what God has for me even if I tried, possessed by the Holy Ghost I can see him in my eyes. Wrestling against my flesh, convicted by the light; I'm losing my mind, there is no rewind only my limited time to live my life under the banner of the most high. Fighting for love is my "why", writing my heart out as I cry, putting my sanity on the firing-line every time.

Harvesting the darkness from my old life to create bread that gives life. Wrapped in all black cutting through demons from my past; a reaper of rhymes they were always outclassed. No need for a mask; I prefer to feel the bloody splash, eyes of a maniac slashing down my fear like a demoniac I'm no longer holding back; strictly comeback, no more falling off horseback; this time I'm breaking the horse's back.

I will not fail, I will show my gratitude for my savior taking those nails, I could be drained pale and still write my words like a nightingale, bringing in pain on the inhale while releasing flames on the exhale; I'm the dragon you've heard about in fairy tales. I have a sonnet etched into every scale, I was born to be a walking telltale, I've always been a mythical creature in mortal shell, how else can you explain how I write this well?

THE GHOST OF POETRY

I'm translucent, flowing in and out of rubrics of thought like fluid, thought I was there; then I'm here, living on a plane of existence reserved for those without fear. A forgotten pioneer lost on the supernatural hemisphere, an unnatural buccaneer sailing on seas you can't see or hear, do you get it yet? I'm the ghost of poetry that's befriended the unknown, an agent from the world of souls.

A reaver for the mysteries, a weaver for the unseen, a mage designed to set minds free. Never fit into any code because I'm a glitch, a walking disruption in the matrix, more complex than a triple helix; you'll find I'm just a mutant with the abilities of a mystic, rising through my limits like a phoenix; an aberration that goes against physics, "how is he doing this?" I have a mind that's mosaic.

Saying I'm crazy only fuels my passion to be amazing at crafting rhymes that seem like an impossibility, yet when I'm added to the equation the probability increases drastically; because like I've been saying: I'm greatness that's gauging the limits of what it means to write poetry. If I could say one thing about me; I couldn't. Can't put a label on something mythic; you shouldn't. So I'll wrap this up by saying if you're thinking about coming against me; I wouldn't.

I'LL WAIT FOR YOU

You may not answer back as fast as I'd like you too; but I guess this is God's way of testing the trust I have for you, looking out the window feeling blue; I don't have a clue if you really love me the way I love you. I wish I could peak inside your head just to make sure I won't be left for dead. If you could see all I've survived then it'd make perfect sense for what I said, I can only pray you won't hurt me the way the others did.

I love you so much it hurts, how I feel about you I can't put into words, it feels like when two eagles merge and dive headfirst and letting go before they hit the earth. That's the trust I'm giving you, this is why I want to know if you'll hold my heart or let it burst, you feel like a blessing and a curse, I shouldn't be expecting the worst; but God only knows why trusting you so much makes my wounds spurt.

I'll wait for you, I find a calm in you, your love maybe riddled with holes like the moon; but like a wolf I'll still call for you. In my heart you'll always have a room, I hope you come soon; because baby I really want it to be you. The one that'll be my sun when nights weigh heavy and the world cuts me open, to be with me in my final moments, please... Let it be your hand I'll be holding.

DEAL WITH THE SANDMAN

Me and the sandman agreed "now is the time to make my dream a reality". Changing what I see by the way I think is a technique I learned while asleep, and now it's become an easy thing to do when walking the streets. Something happens I don't like; suddenly finding myself at a different point in time standing in the blood of a demon that tried to take my life, smile of a crocodile; as I wipe blood from the knife.

In my life I was always underestimated, now I look at others I overestimated and think "you're one bad move away from cremation". I think I'm losing my patience, I think I'm tired of everyone's arrogance, just leave me alone and there won't be a penance, just walk away and there won't be a funeral held for your ignorance. I'm one bad day away from showing them how bad it gets.

Wait… Why am I feeling this? This isn't me, have I lost myself to the technique? Does me wishing an outcome to come into being bring out the monster when I sleep? Wait, did the sandman trick me? I said I wanted my desires when I waked; not to be possessed every time I make a wish when I'm awake, for heaven's sake, now I have be careful what I say; because now I'm closer than ever to being doomsday.

WARTIME

Shattering skulls with a hollow-point, flipping a coin to make the choice, two-face the minute we're talking gunpoint. Hope you saved at the checkpoint, trying to understand your viewpoint; for why you wanna take point against someone who's an endpoint. Don't disappoint; keep walking in the same choice, raise your voice, got my blood pumping from all the noise, don't be a killjoy; time to play boy, just a cowboy messing with a doughboy.

Got my lewis on ready; breath getting heavy. Hit you in the chest harder than a chevy; messy with the warfare; bloody. Begging me for mercy but I already blacked out raging on your body drowning you in the wrath you wanted so badly. Losing our minds to the noradrenaline pumping, barely feel pain with the adrenaline we're consuming, no time for thinking, purely primal movements, funny how all the sudden you no longer want to do this.

What happened man? I thought you were from the badlands?
All that talk just to wind up tied up in the back of a black van,
what? didn't you know?

I'm a bad man...

JESUS CHRIST

There's something about you, and how you speak truth that
causes my spirit not to move, a deeper part of me knows the
answer has always been you. Many see you as just a man who
loved God, they couldn't be more wrong, you're a piece of
The Father that came to show what it means to live according
to your law, you said it's the sinners you came to call.
You said

> *"You shall love the Lord your God, with all*
> *your heart, and with all your soul, and*
> *with all your mind. This is the great and*
> *foremost commandment. The second is like*
> *it. You shall love your neighbor as*
> *yourself, on these two commandments*
> *depend the whole law and the prophets" -*
> *Matthew 22:37-40*

To me this means when you speak the truth; it's in peak
because you're not diluted by worrying about how you'll be
seen. It means when you talk about hell and gnashing of
teeth; you're revealing the life we'll have if it's not your
guidance we're underneath. You love us so much you never
want us out of touch, you want us to live in you "The Vine"
so we can have a life where The Father is glorified, for God is

good all the time.

THE LOST SHEEP

Lost in sin thinking I'm not worthy of living inside your pin, I barely produce the wool to fill the bin. So I ran away in shame with my cowering head, I thought "I'd rather be dead than show my face again". I wandered through valleys black, I crossed rivers where waves crash, I settled myself in the land where I was first saved at; because I believed I was defective and bad.

Weeping in a hole under some rocks while the vultures mock "we knew you were rotten stock". Then suddenly I heard a faint whistle, could it be? My Shepard has come to seek me? I shout from the darkness of my hideout beaten and worn-out, I go to peak my head out and suddenly a wolf tries to take me out, "YOU'RE NOT GOING ANYWHERE NOW!!!" roaring; he starts digging to take me down.

Almost through his paw touches my nose, tears fall as I call louder than ever before "FATHER", suddenly there was a loud cracking of a whip followed by a whimper from the wolf's lips, as he backed out I saw you standing in power and determination; readied to fight staring the devil down. I watched in awe as you effortlessly defeated the cretin. Once it was all said and done you put me on your shoulders and said

"I love you, I knew you were missing"

CRUSADER

Warring against demons has always been my center, clearing out thoughts that puts me at war is what I've been doing since I could swing a sword. Got a quick temper for spirits seeking to devour that I can't stop myself from seeking power. If I'm going to crush armies I need to ground myself straight in the wire, never been one to avoid the fire, smile wide; searing away what makes me a liar, say I'm not doing enough? You're preaching to the quire.

Locked in a cage with my maker to understand what it means to be a son for the empire, a dead stare as I study the mirror. Refining my character to please the one who gave me the chance to live as a warrior. I was made to be a messenger and I won't fail in the only thing I was created to go after, the world covers me in laughter yet I find refuge in my savior, reminding me I shouldn't worry about what the hellhounds murmur.

Full set of armor with a great-sword of fire slashing through monsters seeking to take God's children under, couldn't stop me if they tried; I only get hotter, eyes of a hunter; mind of a master; heart of a lion; voice of thunder; they'll go down witnessing a creation dedicated to The Father. They'll feel what it means to know a crusader, they'll know me by the way I continue to charge through the slaughter.

CERBERUS

Sometime I feel like I have three heads, Cerberus-minded let me explain this: one is happy; the other sad, but the one in the middle is mad. Caught in between worlds; pulled back and forth, tug of war; both sides trying to control the floor. Trying to predict how I'll act is like reaching in a mixed bag, trying to play with me is like hot-potato with a live frag, want to play? I doubt that.

Just like the dog of legend I guard my heart's underworld ruthless, bypassing me now requires ambrosia level access, sweet songs from lyres no longer cut it, if I even hear sweetness; the odds of you escaping unscathed are beyond less. I've been sung into madness, your pretty words are now baseless, one more step closer; you're faceless. Speechless? Good, I've worked hard to hammer out my weakness.

I no longer smile these days, every time I did I was shown why that was a mistake, no longer will I put myself on the stake for people who would never do the same, treated like a game I leveled up the difficulty to "just walk away". I'm focused on me the rest of my days so my advice to you is don't even come my way unless you have something to offer that's worth me opening my gates.

PSYCHO

"Man, you've never been the same, always working no time for games what made you change? Why so deranged? Why you gotta rage, why not relax, just take a day, rest so you can better create?" everyone spits in my face. Get out the way! running to the me that feels the same way. Gotta maximize; gotta realize: tomorrow just might take your life. My oh my, why oh why, do we continue to justify wasted time.

The highest a crime, should be a sign, that reminds you can't rewind, no I'm not fine, no I'm not high, pouring out every single bottle of red-white wine, I want what's mine, only wanna climb, only the best for the rest of my life, I'll walk this knife; walk this strife; lift every weight till it's my time. Every moment an apology to self for not choosing me, I will live free, I will be who I want to see.

"Just a wanna be. A man in a dream, just a waste of space trying to make history". You think your words mean anything? I say darker things, things you couldn't conceive, things that would make you look in the mirror and hate what you see. But I refuse to be like you, just a vessel to be a demons tool, food for evil don't got a clue, just a meat sack doing what it's told to do.

FILLING A VOID

I pace around the room, wanting touch from anyone, wishing I could just have "the one". I'd block out the whole world just to have someone who'd stay all the way through, I would shake the earth with what I'd do if I could just have a love that was true, there wouldn't be a single thing I couldn't move. But angels taunt "you have to become who you want" forcing me to love the one in the mirror nobody wants.

Believing I'll always be alone I let my pleasures overflow "if I can't have someone to share the road then I'll just let go" trying to fill the void with food, games, alcohol, drugs and clothes. But no matter how much I put in the inferno my soul remains hollow, remains hungering after a love that from myself I withhold. How can I hold my own hands when I'm what others can't stand, tell me? How can I love a broken man?

I don't even know who's under the mask. I've hated myself for so long I'm just a mix of what everyone wants, never really protecting myself like I would my love, just crushing my identity into something that can be loved. Why is this so hard? What's so wrong with me I can't love my own heart? Why am I always crying over my scars? Why do I want others to give me my worth? I... understand...

How could anyone love someone that feels like a curse.

THE WAR ON FLESH

There's nothing else to do but break free from chains holding me from who I want to be, "Is this who I want to be? Is what I'm doing what I want to see? Is this thing going to build me?", but it goes so much deeper than that, it can be felt in these words from the past

> "Watch your thoughts, they become your words.
>
> Watch your words, they become your actions.
>
> Watch your actions, they become your habits.
>
> Watch your habits, they become your character.
>
> Watch your character, it becomes your destiny."
>
> - A Wise Man

Do you see? The things in which we put energy gain momentum, that over time can snowball into the size of a colosseum. It's no longer just "one more time", what you're doing can lay claim to your life, every action you make shapes your mind, there is no rewind; you really are fighting for your life, there's everything to gain from no longer abusing your mind,

Think you can stop anytime? Try…

A LONELY SOUL

Peering out his tinted window; he watches a family take their stroll.

As parents slip their fingers into a hold; he feels his heart has a hole.

Watching the family laugh and play; hoping "that'll be me someday".

Dad making soft wrestling rolls as mom snaps it on the camera roll,

Moments; he thinks are better than any TV show,

Beautiful; how together they make a rainbow,

Captivated; that in each other they found a home,

Wishing; they'll forever hold on and never let go.

"I hope they know how lucky they are to have someone to hold"

Holding their wonderful life in his head; he says "I hope so,

Not a single day gos by without me looking out this window;

Just so I can catch some of the joy falling off their shadows"

And as sorrow took hold; he wept the tears of a lonely soul.

A SPECTER

A specter; battered

His mind; shattered.

The heart; tattered.

Name; Does it matter?

As he walks; finds others lost,

Seeing himself; pays a cost.

Betrayed; takes the loss,

Numb; holds the frost.

Never asked for much,

Just a gentle touch,

Yet; is discarded like mulch.

Found; on the edge of a gulch.

Swinging his feet

"No one would miss me"

Pondering Death's mystery

He stands up and starts leaning.

Wanting to be free he steps.

Finally "I'm falling",

Closing his eyes

Smiling.

You know nobody,

Be kind to somebody,

We're all in pain over something,

The world won't change if we do nothing.

Pain is what makes us family.

THE PAIN OF THE PAST

I remember, how I would fold like rubber, a lover so broken I handed my heart to liars. Used, abused, and left for the fire; I let their actions define my character, believing I was less than the cost of my mirror; my reflection turned into horror, allowing others pain brushes to paint my picture. I became what I most hated to satisfy what was narrated. Back then I won't lie I was curious, immersed myself in sins most devious, "why not if everyone says I'm this".

And I was for awhile, I went completely wild, for the first time in a long time I felt like a child, but that's all I was "a child". Leaving behind my responsibilities for my own un-lived fantasies. I regret nothing; I got it all out of me. The rebel who thought he knew better, the sinner who thought without God he could be happier, the lover who thought true love could be found in godless hours.

Living outside the bounds of hands that could actually repair what was causing my despair; I eventually crashed out of thin air when I saw the same pattern in a different square. That's when I surrendered my life, that's when I realized "I have no idea how to get my desired mind", so now I keep my flesh denied to keep myself from falling back into the pigsty of thinking "I know how to become a butterfly" when without the divine I'm just a dog digging for lies.

MANDELA EFFECT

In 2008 they turned on the large hadron collider (LHC) where they were smashing atoms, in 2009 the Mandela effect was first coined by Fiona Broome. Since then, there has been a large collective phenomenon where certain events and things are remembered differently, most notoriously the peanut butter 'jiffy' that never existed technically.

Or how about how 'toons' were only ever 'tunes', what about how "Luke, I am your father" was only ever "No, I am your father", or how "we are the champions" never actually ended with the lines "of the world". It's not your mood I'm trying to spoil, I'm trying to prove how after the collider it seems we shifted into a timeline not familiar.

This is why it's only God I fear, in Matthew 13:36-43; Jesus compares the kingdom of God to a man sowing good seed (righteous) and an enemy sowing weeds (unrighteous) and how when harvest comes separated they'll be. One gos into the barn and the other fire, so based off our actions and heart; we could hypothetically be shifted into a dark world we don't desire.

A LOVE NOT FORGOTTEN

Covered in shadow alone

I find your memory has crept into my soul.

The passage of time doesn't lie,

You still cause tears to come upon my eyes.

The love we once shared

Still holds true;

In a heart that could never forget

You.

You may have forgotten me

And that's fine,

It shows how some love

Is only ever felt on one side.

The moments I had with you

Is something scarce,

I'm happy you were the one

By whom they were shared.

We might be far apart,

You may have sealed away

From me parts of your heart.

But you will always be remembered

As a beautiful star.

YOU KNOW

This isn't so bad, life and all that,

Think about how sad is actually

Just happy pretending to be bad,

Did you smile? I hope so, you deserve that.

We can be so dramatic sometimes

Like how I am when I write these lines

"EVERYTHING DEPENDS ON THIS LINE!!!"

Really? Honestly I think my crowd will think it's fine.

Taking everything so seriously I forget to smell the roses too,

Have I found peace? Did I accidentally fall in love with you?

This far into the book it's safe to say we've both flipped our lid.

You're the love of my dreams, no judgement, just us we're chilling with.

They'll never understand us, that's fine, I hope not,

Then we'd just be like the rest of the sandlot,

Lets throw them for a loop, lets show them the power of "boop",

Just from that line you should know we have the masses duped.

So let's be weird and show them the power of our crew.

A BROKEN MAN

What happened to you?

"What happened to me?"

I know you see it too.

"What do you mean?"

The fire in your eyes has lost its light.

"It's all useless, money is meaningless."

You're right, but this is about your life.

"Don't you get it? Nothing is timeless."

So you give up? Just ending it by being a drunk?

"Everything I work for will just be taken away."

My God, you really did give up your faith.

"They're all the same, only loved for what you can pay."

Even if that's true, this life was given to you.

"What if I just want to waste away?"

That's a lie, you want to see the best you.

"Maybe I don't, maybe I just want to cave."

And be a repeat of what's wrong with everyone today?

"That's low. I didn't ask to be broke, they chose."

Blaming others for who you became? Just a pawn in their game?

"WHY DO I HAVE TO CARRY THE LOAD!?! WHY CAN'T I FOR ONCE BE THE ONE SOMEONE CHOSE!!!"

Because then you'd never choose to become whole.

THE REAL YOU

The darkness in my head sings sweet songs of death.

Whispers of "this and that" judgements cast by the past.

Am I still dead? I feel my shadow's breath on my neck.

I escape the black just to be reminded of the scars on my back.

Everyone wants resurrection from death to living

But nobody tells you how the lid to your coffin is heavy,

Or how you'll be digging through the mistakes of your history

To reach an understanding from where you can redefine your story.

The old you and your new identity will always be warring,

Fighting against impulses you thought were dead and buried

And I'll tell you right now it's exhausting, you'll wish for peace

But won't find any, Always fighting to become who you want to be.

It's worth it however, to survive the back-to-back winters

Is to truly treasure your new heart when it begins to flower.

What else is worth doing? Tell me. What else is there to do

Other than becoming the real you.

DARK CLOUDS

I wake to a rope around my nape,

Caged by willow branches

I see the trunk is etched in curses.

By my own words I'm choking.

Who knew you could become what you've spoken,

From words broken I turned myself into fruit rotten,

The devil has poured me a lake of bourbon below

So even if I escape the gallows; I'll drown in my sorrows.

I look out to the dark clouds

And through the thunderclouds

A voice shakes the very ground

"BY YOUR OWN WORDS

YOU ARE BOUND"

A DARK TRUTH

In bitter cold; a dark truth unfolds,

That only God fully loves your soul.

You find how much you are truly alone,

How nobody cares about your empty home.

Blood may be thicker than water

But in the end you'll see how that love

Is limited when weighed against their own coffers.

They're not you and never were, they lie for what you offer.

You can still have a big heart,

Just know some love needs to be dark,

You can't keep splitting yourself apart,

How is that fair to your own heart?

Nobody will love you like you,

And you know I speak the truth,

So just get it over with,

Just start falling back in love

With you.

THE ANSWER FOR LIFE

It's a Gift for You.

HEY

Hey, you can come out now, I see you by the door, little me creeping around. You don't have to bite your tongue, let it all out; I promise I won't judge. You may be sporadic, so much so some say you're erratic, but that's what makes you so electric. It's fine if they hide in a cell to satisfy what others deem acceptable, but it's just you and me versus the world, don't ever think you're expendable.

I'm sorry it took so long to love you. How can I be so stupid that I didn't see the best lover looking back at me. I've always wondered if my reflection had speech; what would you speak? I mean, I know we'd talk, but would you be my better half? Would you hold me when I break like glass? Would you play games with me and laugh? I think so, I think you'd remind me "it's me and you till the end of the show!"

I truly believe you'd do that for me because you're just me behind a reflective screen. And I know who I am, I'd give my heart away to help another stand, and that in itself is just the kind of man I am. Ashes to ashes, dust to dust, the only thing that truly lasts is the seeds I've sown in the name of love, but of course you know that, for you've been my very best friend since day one.

SOME JUST HURT

They lash out to defend a child inside who was always beat down for "being to bright", at some point in their life; something dark shattered their mind. If only you could see, how their own mother hit her babies, or how the father sacrificed their needs for drinking, maybe if we could see the scars others hide underneath we wouldn't be so quick to curse them to hades.

Wishing them to burn in hell; when life forced them to make that shell. Some just hurt, some hurt so bad there's no love left to give anymore, this is why giving the opposite action instead of the expected reaction is so important, some people are just in a state of constant mourning; and by you giving love you warm them like the morning.

Eye for eye, tooth for tooth, all of that wrath just spills back onto you. What if it was you? Losing your family then fired and treated like dogfood? There would be a pain so thick that of course it would make your soul bitter and sick, we're all trying to live; but death is found in seeking revenge. Sure some violence makes sense, but how can you ask to be forgiven when you've not given forgiveness.

MAYBE I'M NOT THE BEST

Sure, I may not be the best, but someway somehow I have to get these thoughts outside my head. I cry a lot, plot twist; I shed so many tears so I don't slit my wrists. Translating what's in my heart is so hard; a part of me wants to throw in the towel and go back to the dark. But I won't, I refuse, just the idea of the old me makes me want to puke.

Going back to wallow in vomit I left; I can't lie I'd actually choose death. I may not be the best, I already know, stop making my one regret the bullet you load to shoot my soul, stop making all my flaws your own personal sideshow. Why hate me? What's so wrong about my dream? I just want my art to be somebody's healing.

I may be broken, I may not be the best one to be chosen; but I'm doing my very best to be worthy of the gift I'm holding. Having a point of view is a blessing; why belittle others for having a different perspective? I believe your voice should be free; just don't use yours to try and silence me, "I won't let anyone hurt you" I already promised,

I won't stand for you insulting the new character I've harnessed.

SAYING GOODBYE

If I should die before I wake

I pray the lord my soul to take.

But should you catch me on the ground

I'm happy I got to see your face.

You are the only one I wanted near

Before I take the hand of death,

To give everything I have left to give,

A kiss sealed with my dying breath.

No one will ever know

Just how deep

Our love actually goes,

Or ever see how we are me.

This isn't goodbye,

This is hello,

Without death we could never

Enter into forever's fold.

WHY FREE WILL?

Many a man wishes for God to take away lust, they say "If I say in Jesus name you must". No, that's not how it works, the Holy Spirit helps the sores but it's you who must pick up the sword. You say that isn't fair? What is your love worth if you can't choose the other? Free will is why we're special dear. Imagine if you couldn't, just a mindless obedient servant; who's only purpose is to listen, no emotion, strictly a toy to be moved moment to moment.

Some say they would want that so "I can stop being a sinful rat", to have God force them to pick up the slack; as a way to save them from their own trap, but what kind of life is that truly? It isn't one, you become a something of mere puppetry, on this "path" you have no growing character, just a perfect reflection of what God wants you to mirror, in wanting to be a perfect picture you've turned our God into a tyrannical dictator.

You could live 1000 years and still fall short of what God called you to do here. You'll never be perfect; and that's alright, as long as you see why it's so important we need Christ's graceful light. We're all just sinners and I'm no better, I could look into the eyes of a killer and still call him brother. I've put down what's "right" in the eyes of man, I just want you to understand the depth of forgiveness God wants us to have.

LOVE IS PAIN

I just want to be loved,

And I know you do too,

To just once be the one

That hears the words "I love you".

The act of holding another close

Is to open the door to blissful pain,

Where the heart loses all repose

And puts all we own at stake.

What a beautifully dangerous thing,

A rose with the nature of a grenade,

They may pull the pin and make the sting

But for true love; that's the price to be paid.

Worth every moment,

Worth… Being broken.

OUR TEARS

You matter, every drop of water counts, don't you see? It's you we still need. Not one is perfect, that's why your story is so profound, with every misstep, you learn why it's important to stand your ground. This is our first time alive, we all have horror, and finding your "why" is the gold everyone is mining for. Our minds are constantly at war with comfort and becoming more, we want character but try to haggle the price on the key to that door.

"Why is it so high?", anything worth having isn't the cheapest thing in the store, a great life where your heart, soul, and mind are unified means to sacrifice the lies holding you from the light. Die to the vices, they're just distractions, pain is the way, embrace now is the time to change, accept others will spit, you remind them there's a better way to live. It's always been your life, don't get to the end just to wish you didn't give your power to the hive.

The horses we call our emotions can be tamed; It's true, nothing is more beautiful than soul wrestling with the reigns to control "you". It gives hope, faith even, that "if they can find control then I can also take hold", Isn't powerful? How the way you sow inspires others to grow. We can't defeat death, but we can be purposeful with every breath, sounds to easy? Maybe it is, maybe we make things harder on purpose, maybe we don't celebrate the little wins because if we did;

We'd find out the whole time we were holding ourselves back from greatness. And that's a shame many don't want to deal with when it should only be guilt for the wasted actions and not self-defecation for being imperfect.

WHY DO YOU HATE YOURSELF?

I've never seen anything more beautiful, why do you hate the colors inside yourself? You're different; and I think it's high time you accepted it. I know you didn't ask to be a rainbow, didn't ask to be the star of the show, but from your shine you help heal parts in others that are broke. You really are a walking dream, you weave hope into the hearts of those that feel unseen, how can you not see?

That without you; it's much harder to believe that love can exist outside of "personal need". You may not be perfect but you're perfectly you, I hope you know that I tip my hat to the courage you have; and that's the truth. It's never easy being the outcast others point to for a laugh, but laugh harder, they'll never experience what it means to be a trail-blazer, trapped forever in an invisible cell labeled: "Proper".

You'll always be "crazy" for having the audacity to live outside your shell, to ask the hard questions about 'self', to recreate what it means to be "yourself", this life has never been about material wealth, it's always been about leaving with a smile, to know you didn't waste a single drop in your inkwell. Where every letter, every stroke of the pen, was written with willful intent, where you're proud to say with your final breath

"What a great life, I'm ready for death."

A WALK IN SILENCE

So much noise, screens riddling our minds with disease, not a moment for ease, robbing peace, promising answers for why we feel like a broken piece. Speakers blaring motivational speech, trying to set others free by screaming what we already know underneath, we wear our shame like a decorative wreath; as we showcase why we can't achieve our dreams, decreasing our value further from the words we speak.

We never consider maybe it's time for a glass of water, maybe it's time for that walk we're so afraid to wander, no chatter, just a time for reflection to ponder why we no longer see the world with wonder. When did it happen? When did we lose sight of the destination we mapped when we still dreamed of being our own captain? Was it all the pleasures we drowned ourselves in? Is that when we gave in?

Was it when we first failed that we accepted "I'm just a normal human"? We gave up so easy, surrounded by the doubts of our own family mixed with the shame of thinking we're a broken thing from failing; that we limited ourselves to what we believe is achievable for "me". You don't even know who "you" are, of course you're not yet a star, no one starts as the master, it's from cultivating your spark where you find why it's so hard.

You find that your value is made from the story of how you healed your scars.

I FELL AGAIN

I fell so far, did so well just to put myself back behind bars, but I won't stop. There's no way I'll stay in this grave, I'll dig through this shame, I refuse to be lost in my old ways. My heart craves the familiar but the mind knows pleasure is a liar, a short term trap to put long term virtues under wraps. I know I may not be who I want to be yet, but if I continue to invest; then my actions will eclipse my inner debt.

Working through self-doubt is learning to trust yourself again after breaking your word, we have to want to not be like this anymore. I'm talking to myself: "Jackie, soon we exit the floor, soon we won't be able to open the doors, they're right there, please change, please, be more". If there was ever a time to go to war for the life we're after then now is the time to be a warrior, now is the time to pick up the sword.

We may fall, we may still have an identity that has holes in its walls, but the longer we stall; the more we ignore the family waiting for us to answer the call. Yes, we are broken, battered, shattered, maybe homeless, but one things for sure: we're chosen. Not soldiers; but captains, our tests are harder because we can handle it, God knows what to give us in order to maintain what will be given, have faith,

YOU'RE GOING TO MAKE IT!!!

BECOMING YOU

In the dark part of our heart; is a place we release pain from our eyes, where everything is covered in moonlight, where tears become butterflies and take flight; sailing into the sea of night we call our mind. Grief is the crucible of true love, can't feel true pain without feeling "one", whether it's with yourself or with someone, to rip apart what was; for some outside cause is enough for pause.

You thought people were nice; then they weren't, you thought being kind was enough; then you were hurt, you thought they loved you; then were burned, you thought you loved yourself; then turned. When tears are shed it's your heart begging to understand "why is this the direction that's being tread?", a question that's only answered inside your own head.

Wanting everything under the sun; thinking it makes you someone is a lie told by our instincts for a millennia, "broken" is allowing another to fill the holes we call "us", mom, dad, brother, sister, strangers, cousins, all people we stuff into our worth of self to fill up the parts we think we can't fill up because we aren't "enough". Let's sit down, let's grab a mirror and be proud we're the only one around, it's okay to grieve,

But don't attach your self-worth to anything that destined to one day leave.

LET IT ALL GO

All the emotion tied to our lack of movement has to be tossed in the ocean, the broken beliefs have to be cracked wide open.

Leave it, don't you see? These are the dead parts we're supposed to bury. These are the chains we were trained to believe "this is how to behave". All the judgements, projections and "corrections" have to be filtrated back into what's most important: your decision.

You didn't have a choice when you were younger, forced to listen or beaten, "DO AS I SAY!!!" Or mistreated, fall in line or abandoned. But now it's all different, now you're older; and they're still hoping the "baby" elephant won't pull the stick up and escape the "ringmasters". They trained you like an obedient pit-bull, treated like a slave so you'll chase their validation and praise; what bull.

They're afraid of you no longer accepting the roles they chained to your name. You can do it, accept it, this is it, the only life you'll ever get, don't let anyone dictate "your place" in all this. It's time to wake up, it's time to fill up your own cup, don't get yourself stuck in the lies they've spun, a fly to a web; is what they want, so what will you do?

I hope you get up.

I ?

Who is 'I'?

What am 'I'?

Why is 'I' alive?

How is 'I' inside?

Where can I find 'I'?

What is the life of 'I'?

Is 'why' the reason for 'I'?

'I' cry, 'I' laugh, 'I' die?

Why?

Death?

Breath?

A ride?

Maybe

'I'

Is

Why.

THIS WORLD

The longer I walk the more I don't want to talk, each time it gets heavier; the striking hand on the clock, "tick-tock" it laughs and mocks. Small talk has turned into mindless trash, there's a deep cut on my heart; a gash. The cast it's wrapped with is covered by blackness from others that keep coming to sign it, the ink seeps through and stains my heart; written by: "a friend", hurts all the more when they stab me in the dark.

Love here is always conditional "can they increase my odds for survival?", I found people not letting God chisel their marble are just intelligent animals, and an animal will kill its own to have their needs fulfilled. You truly are alone when you're trying to find your way back home, it's so the wrong people don't rob the vault when you become gold, this journey to be whole will cut away your eyes stone and show you some people just want to freeload.

Did that make you sad? I hope so, it means you're here for more than just that, you desire something that makes others mad because they know it's what everyone should be chasing after at. The "why". To refine one's mind to a way of life that makes them feel alive, to cultivate knowledge and harvest wisdom to make the finest inner brine, so no matter what happens to you in this world of lies; you'll know the truth of 'yourself' from the way you sowed your time.

HOW TO SEE DIFFERENTLY

My love for this world is almost unbearable, this love doesn't come from a broken mental lens, it comes from a creed of how I live. "I wish more people loved" so I do, "I wish they'd let their real self shine through" so I dress like a cockatoo, "I wish they understood we're all a part of a bigger 'you'" so I treat everyone like myself, someone gives me hell; I walk away from that old version of myself.

I love so very deeply, including me, it's not fair to me if I stick around to let someone belittle me, we would never let that happen to who we call family; so why do we stay knowing we'll get angry? Do we stay to hear the things we believe about ourselves? Probably. Longing to have something outside affirm the lies we weave that keep us from living free. The truth is you're still writing, so focused on on old chapters you forget you're still working on act three.

The truth is, I was in so much pain internally I couldn't bear another day believing I would never be happy, "if it happened for them, then it can happen for me" is still the leading force in becoming who've I've always wanted to be. Just reading about others changing their lives that were off worse; inspired my thoughts to take a different course, and they all said the same thing: "I couldn't keep being a victim of war".

Everything I've said is a result of my choice to find life instead of death, and I'm so happy I kept the path of where God led.

WHAT IS?

What is art really? But metaphors and symbols making a symphony.

What is Poetry? But the words of soul painting a subjective reality.

What is music? But alchemy of angels weaving sheets into our being.

What is life? But the journey of a single soul becoming whole.

What is love? But the sacrifices of one to ensure life in another.

What is a lover? But two spirits sharing the feeling of pleasure.

What is true love? But two wholes choosing eternity together.

What is love? But the sacrifices of "self" for the one in the mirror.

What is purpose? But the set instructions of reaching your wishes.

What is your passion? But the one interest you MUST live with.

What is indecision? But wasting time for fear of painful progress.

What is pain? But a device that brings the sense of fulfillment.

What is Life? But the present moment.

A MIND OF BROKEN GLASS

A mind made from broken glass will always see the cracks, stitching on patches of the past; they break themselves upon the rock of "fact". Yelling "I did this and that, you can't say I'm not a miserable rat!!!" as they pile on more trash, isn't sad? So caught in the delusion that we're still the same person that used to be under the illusion that we forget we're human. And humans have an amazing ability to change from moment to moment.

You did the best you could with what you knew, "how do I become loved and valued?" so you became a fool, no family member worth looking up to; you became something useful: a tool. And you worked hard, oh yes you did, got all of the validation and praise you were starved of as a kid, being the best helper in every situation, letting boundaries be broken because all you felt was a "someone" is finally giving you attention.

Left alone for so long and treated like a freak you thought "I must be what's wrong" so you broke yourself into something you thought others would get along. Bent your unique shape out of shape to appease the insecurities of those projecting their own pain; you forgot you're the one holding the controller to your own game, I wish you wouldn't carry so much shame for the sakes of others who won't even remember your name.

I think it's time to change, to paint yourself with colors you create; rather than what others try to narrate, their confidence is misplaced if they try to dictate "how and why" you behave, because now:

No one will ever again… Take away YOUR name.

BAD DREAMS

I believe dreams is how God talks, last night I walked to places and people I shouldn't of, he sent nightmares as His way of saying "enough son". He sees the death and decay. Sent a warning ahead so I won't go back to being dead, to stay on the right side of the fence, it's time and I know it, it's time for repentance, to beg God for forgiveness, to let the old fall to ashes, to surrender my destructive habits; to be resurrected as a phoenix.

I'm not mad he sent demons, I'm not mad he gave me a glimpse of my coming apocalypse, I went back drinking, I went back smoking, I went back to things I shouldn't be doing, and as result? What's a Father to do but grab his belt and bring hell to save his child falling under a dark spell. The very same spell craft that used to drag me all over the mat, a way of life that's far away from where heaven is at.

I'm the one in the wrong, it's time to answer for what I've done, there's no more room for error, time to throw all of it in the fire, all the darkness that chains my spirit like barbwire. I'm so sick of being a coward, the vomit is still the same flavor: wasted hours. This is it, I give it to you lord, please destroy the hold these powers have tried to root in my character, renew my mind and create in me my heart's desire: a new creature.

A LETTER TO ME

Dear Me,

We haven't talked in awhile; is everything alright? I hope you still got that smile of light, I pray you're trying to stick to that dream you told me about that night, I wish you all the best wishes all the time, you're that one star this world needs to stay alight. You're that one fighter this world needs more than ever, I know you're feeling tired; but aren't we all carrying a fire that needs to reach a pyre?

They need you, you know it's the truth, so many unloved souls waiting to meet you, don't deny them the gift of meeting the best you, to light something in them in a way only you can do, with something the Holy Spirit gave you: a pure heart refined through-and-through. You always say: "be what you want to see" so right now I need you to stand here with me, take a deep breath, just breathe, it'll be okay, trust me.

You'll have that great life and family, children laughing and running, able to help the needy through charity, a beacon of love in a world filled with misery, but you have to stand, you have to be a man, you have to be the father we never had, time to be a dad, time to leave all the childish toys in the past, it's high time we take our life back, to long have we been sidetracked, let's get back on track, now come on!

I'll race you to the boat where we're crossing over at!!!

DON'T STAY DOWN

WE'RE SLIPPING!!! Quickly! Slam the pick into the icy sheet! Don't give up! We're only a few feet from everything we've ever wanted to be! Do it! break through the screen of disbelief, change, everything is within our reach. They can't stop us now, to far ahead to doubt, hold your head up proud, you answered the call when you heard the the trumpet sound.

The monsters are far below the snow, don't fall back to the ground because it looks like soft snow. There's always a cost, you and I both know the loss isn't worth giving up our cross. It may be heavy but it's necessary to prepare the spirit for heights where it's hard to breathe, where most would get weak in the knees is where you'll show

Philippians 4:13 -

> *"I can do all things through Christ who
> strengthens me"*

We were called because He sees something in us we don't, saved from the lion's throat; we must show why we were the one God chose by the way we carry our stones. Through fire and blood; we will survive the flood, we will get back up, doubling up on rising through the mud; we ignite a deep well of love for being a child of the blessed (bless-id) one.

IF I WAS HAPPY?

What does it even mean? To be happy? I feel like the meaning changed after 19, things weren't as pleasing to have, just "toys, metal and trash", the real things worth having always made me sad. I knew how I felt about myself is what I wanted fixed more than anything else; but fixing yourself is like playing jigsaw with a broken mirror or setting books on an uneasy shelf, eventually it all gos back to hell.

I couldn't do it, no matter how hard I tried, the philosophy, the knowledge, all of it seemed to hold the answer I wanted hostage. Only through personal relations with God did I find what I sought, happy only for moments; then I was not, a revelation that toppled my understanding of happiness with one thought: "without suffering; true happiness wouldn't be possible at all".

It's only from feeling evil do we appreciate the chains of angels, only from living wild do we find value in peace and quiet, only by hiding do we allow God to show us we're worth finding. So am I happy? Yes, more than ever, for the first time in my life I now know the reason for why we suffer, because the laughter coming after wouldn't mean a thing if we were "happy" forever.

I'M SCARED OF RISING

Lord, this poem is long over due, I regret for being so far away from you. Calling my name over valleys and hills; yet from my lips are found with drops of swill, I've always been ill, how can a man like me serve your will? I don't even feel worthy of the Holy Spirit by which I'm filled. I've never believed I've ever truly had a great mind, why don't you see I'm just a lie? Yet tears fall from your eyes calling me to the light.

But I did cry out, I did beg for a life in which I can be proud, so shattered and beaten down; that when I prayed it was more pain than sound, but you heard the silent cries from my heart aching to fall down. As I laid dying you called me from my coffin; and the only offering I had to offer was a heart going rotten, yet you smiled, yet you hugged my spirit like a lost child. You said "don't worry, we'll save it… I promise".

God please forgive me, Jesus please love me, Holy Spirit please hold onto me, I've never been what you're telling me I'm worthy of being. I'm sorry I destroy myself to show you how "I'M JUST COWARD WHO DOESN'T DESERVE HELP!!!". I'm coming out the tomb, baptism is being made new like when a baby comes from the womb, I'm holding onto everything I heard from you, from now on it's just me and you, how could it be any other way?

I mean, the only reason I'm here is because of you.

IT HURTS

Sometimes when I write there's pain dripping from my fingertips, a guitarist of the pen; my heart is cut on strings of memories that tempt "let it end, all the time you've wasted, such a fool, you're better off amongst the ghouls". Linings of truth cut like a hot wire, there's a reason when the devil speaks he uses fire, all the things we know need to be cast in the pyre; are the keys he uses to hotwire our mind away from our Father, he uses truth to make us malleable enough to manipulate disaster.

This is why you can't play both sides, we start to hate ourselves because the devil has a point, right? So as long as we're trying to cast off sins of the night; he can't say we're not doing what's right. As long as we fight and feel guilt, as long as we still get embarrassed wallowing in filth, as long as we still feel convicted by our Father's will, can we truly maintain our composure and say "the devil is trying to get us to drink his swill".

So fight, so do what's right, otherwise the lie becomes the spear that pierces your side. It was never supposed to be an easy season, its always been fighting against the animal inside tempting us to treason. Always remember, that is the reason, to escape the impulses that lead to death and prison, it's why the Bible is so important, the only relic holy enough to rewire our heart's cortex; because we know that THIS book IS the way to get through our exodus.

THE POWER OF KNOWLEDGE

It's scary to know somebody is chasing something they deem more important than anything, some just strictly study the inner workings of humanity to bring a desired reality into fruition from the knowledge they cultivated internally, that is something of nightmares and it's truly terrifying. The fact they search for absolute universal truths to manipulate the world under their boot; should be enough for anyone to start studying human patterns too.

There are people that see and treat "love" like a game table, and if you fall for their premeditated fable; you only prove that you were the perfect mark for their carnal journal. This is why it's so important to seek God, they can only manipulate minds drenched in primal sin, but if you hold yourself to boundaries and principles; then you negate the effects of their blackwater spells because you know yourself.

There may be people who use knowledge as a manipulating weapon; but you can use it to find out early on who has the heart of a villain. Everyone is chasing something and I don't blame the snakes for slithering, I blame the ignorance of sheep believing every smile is friendly, but you know what's crazy? Just from me speaking on these things you've already painted me as one of the fiends; when really I'm revealing their secrets so you don't become demon feed.

BRICKS OF LIFE

I remember it, when I first saw children hungry and homeless, riddled with diseases while the rich laughed "good riddance", I couldn't believe it. Standing witness to the evil within; I hit my knees and vowed "I'll never be like them". But now I see why they step on humanity and why they feel no sympathy, they were taught at a young age to carry themselves differently, they were told "they're nothing more than animals, that's why they're in the peasantry".

Everything here is always competitive, and if you outwork the competition then you have rights to lay claim to any reality you wish to live in. Be it "I'm the best there is" or "my best is for the kids", the actions after success will determine the kind of world you'll live in, and if you're strictly "me vs. you" rather than "me and you"; the world has a funny way of making sure you find out why being to self-absorbed makes you a fool.

Whether you're surrounded by people just like you or your wealth is stored up just to have it ripped from you, life will make sure you reap the fruits of the trees you've planted over time. This is why I choose to be humble and kind because one day "how they live may one day be mine". So I give, so I lift, so I help the people who may one day help my kids, life is to short to not want love as the leading aspect for why you draw breath.

What better way to live than to lay bricks that add to life instead of death?

YOU COULD NEVER !!!

No one can separate me from God, even if I walk with the wrong lot; it won't be long before my Father reveals the dogs. Do you hate me for saying that? I hate myself for being that. I've always been, there's never been a time where I didn't eventually crave sin, never was there a time where I was the perfect man. But God loved me regardless, and every time I sin; what I do to His feelings isn't harmless.

It's like watching your own child drink poison, feeling love laced with disappointment; He works out how he'll bring you through the consequences. "They'll get through this" He says with sorrow in His head "WHY WOULDN'T THEY LISTEN!!!" the pain escapes His chest "AM I NOT ENOUGH FOR THEM TO LISTEN TO MY DIRECTION!!! I GAVE THEM LIFE! ONLY I CAN HEAL THEIR HEART THAT'S BROKEN!!!"

We're all His children, if you think it's personal or you've been "targeted", I believe the pain will shape you into someone somebody needs, I believe you could become the angel another needs, I believe you could be greater than you could ever conceive, but only if you're willing to let God help you forge that pain into a masterpiece. Everybody eventually leaves, the only true love you have is He, He's the only Father you'll ever need.

The only validation you'll ever need, don't you see? You're enough because He made sure that your heart still beats.

OVERTHINKING

The black hands of thinking, can squeeze the soul for daydreaming, believing "this would be to much for 'me'"; it isolates and encapsulates mistakes to "save" you from "another mistake". Frustrating; that in seeking change you must find the keys to your chains, escaping the cage you made to keep you safe; means opening doors to views you once called "insane", the "fall from grace" is really just angels moving you to the right place.

We fell. From broken shells we begged the light to set free from all spells, screams of "SAVE ME FROM THIS HELL!!!" are etched on the tears of a child controlled by fear; who now seeks true love in the heart of their Maker. And it will be done, as sure as the rising sun, nothing is required, listen for instruction, the minute you hear "NOW" or "RUN" you do so without hesitation. Do not worry about the "how's", only rely on the promise "it's already figured out".

You're God's child now, nothing will harm you, trust in the direction spirit calls you. Trust, you will be guided out, don't doubt. Fight against the voices trying to coerce you into worser choices, don't drink the poison when you've already been given the victory, they're just making noises. The only thing they can do is lie; hoping you'll abandon the new life God made for you away from the devil's pigsty. So don't leave, LOOK!!!

THE SEA IS PARTING!!! YOU WEREN'T FORSOOK!!!

SELF HATRED

Screaming "WHY!!!" As I stare beyond the sky; I find self-love is the hardest to find. What I've done stains me like lashes from the sun, how can I escape it? The evils I called fun. Feeling hope is lost I play to the tune of my old song; yet my strings collapsed from the weight of knowing it's wrong. Seems I've hit the ceiling, seems I can't play along to the lies I was once feeding, dark patches with skin deep stitching; I found were actually leeches I used to patch the bleeding.

It hurt to much to know I was just fool who fell for translucent smoke, that what seemed obvious to most; I fell for like a joke. I needed something, ANYTHING, to distract me from the holes in my soul, a sinking ship; I packed bowls, popped pills and bottles to escape the work of becoming whole. Instead of developing an understanding that would build me; I chose what was easy, I chose to numb my insecurities instead of looking for wisdom that would bring me serenity.

It's hard to cut away tumors when you see yourself as the cancer, drowning to the bottom of a bottle is the only answer for a soul who's forgotten they matter. Doctoring sorrows in the only way they know how; they destroy themselves with words others sound because they've beaten down their reflection to that of a mouse. Letting rats judge them for the same reason they crush themselves into the ground: they sound exactly like the voices in their head when they lay down.

Some may use sadness to stay in madness, but some are just lost in destructive habits because no one took the time to say "you're worth it". So when you see the twinkle in their eyes that says "I'm hopeless, nobody wants my brokenness" please tell them about

Christ, Jesus.

CHASING DRAGONS

Inside my head

"Just want release, I just want to feel something other than this frustrating 'better me', there are so many steps; who would really care if I took 'a dip', I know God wouldn't want this; but I wouldn't have to if I had someone to kiss. No, I'm wrong, this is exactly why He's kept me away from her all along, what happens when she no longer fits the pedestal I put her on? That's just it, only He knows. And probably what He sees is a broken boy looking for anyone to hold my soul.

But I don't care anymore, I need this fix; to trade the pain of present for the bliss of the past, I mean, I deserve it. I'm not like my old self where I'll go back to living in trash, why can't I? Take a break from lashing my back. Sure it might be a trap, sure the devil may laugh, sure I may lie about what I want once the actions are had; but I have no one to hold but the cross on my chest and I'm fed up with my only reward being 'a better head'. Maybe this isn't me, just demons trying to pull me back down to death

But right now I need meds, right now, no one can save me from numbing myself in bed. It hurts to much to look in the mirror and see everything I'm not, it hurts to be blindfolded not knowing how far I've got to walk, all I want right now is a dragon to take me to the other side of this monumental wall and just for a moment experience a piece of the peace promised to me if I keep walking with the all-mighty God. Please forgive me, I'm sorry for being a pig, but right now I just want to feel some kind of 'kiss'."

THE BOY WITH NO FACE

A boy born without a face came to the sandbox to play, but when he got near all the kids ran in fear. He only wanted to play, he didn't understand why they ran away. He went to the mirror and saw he didn't look like anyone, "maybe this is why they run in fear", so he made a plan to change how he appears. Everyday he'd memorize the popular kid's ways, took note of every crack, wrinkle, and dot on his face, "I will be accepted to play" he would murmur while putting notes on the page.

Later that night while everyone slept; he spent the whole night practicing from the notes he kept. Grabbing at different paints and hues he said "I'm going to look just like the most popular kid at school". As he tried with all his might to get every crevice and line right; he'd romanticize how he'd finally be allowed to "have playtime!!!". He went to sleep dreaming about how tomorrow will be the best day, how "finally I'll get to play!!!"

He got up, got dressed and headed to the sandbox where everyone was playing pick-up-sticks, with his new face he yelled "look!!! I'm just like him!!! Can I play with?", they picked up their sticks and screamed "IT'S HIM!!!" and drove the boy away. As all the colors and ink dripped off his face from the tears that came; he looked into the mirror at the twisted paint and went into a rage, "NOBODY LOVES YOU!!! WHO COULD EVER LOVE A BOY WITH NO-FACE!!!"

PATHETIC

Pathetic mouse, wasting away on the couch, crying over the realization you have to workout or suffer the disease that will permeate if you choose to stay down. There is no escape, it's too late, you've been grabbed by the hands of fate. You've been chosen to carry the burden of heightened awareness, you'll embrace pain or be tortured by the knowledge of the coming furnace for lack of actions. Do you hate this? Do you hate me for being honest? Good, use the hatred to create something other than the fruits of a decaying carcass.

I know you're tired of being a cow. I know you know death comes sooner to those who defile the body with poisons offered by the devil, you can pretend you don't see the anvil but that doesn't stop you from feeling the weight shackled to your ankle. Go on, try to move to the top with all that manure you choose to keep falling back on. X plus Y equals: Z, the past plus you equals: deadman walking. The way this world is designed forces you to comply, certain formulas in life never change, "you want this? Then become the equal [=] sign."

You've been given everything you need, it's up to you to provide the innovative thinking. How many times do you have to hear "no one's coming to save you" for you to become the person needed to complete the equation? What's wrong? Are you deaf or something? Do we need to spoon feed you the same answers you've already reaped? Are you just a baby who needs help because "I'm just to weak"? How can you even ask to marry somebody when you don't even have the will to work for anything?

Final warning, change or stay buried.

I'M RIGHT HERE

I never left you Jackie, I've always been here, I always wanted you in my arms away from the monster, yet you turn from me, saying 'you know better'. And I let you, I let you walk away for the same reason I let you stay, I love you 'J', it cuts deeper than any blade when you choose to drink the same poison after the antidote I gave, what happened? The moment you were healed; for a couple of months you were filled with zeal, but when I began to peel away the shell making you ill; you curse "this wasn't the deal!!!". You know my love is one of transformation, isn't that why you called my name? To save you from your painful situation?

I want to give you your new place but I can't allow you to keep making the same messes all over the place. If you're going to be inside my Father's house you have to be a well trained lion; not an undisciplined mouse. I'm trying to heal you but you keep running back to the devil's dogfood. I'm turning you into a representative for the kingdom, you must learn to obey without needing a reason, you need to trust everything I say is for your own well-being. So by the time I say "it's time to act" you'll be able to make our Father's will come to pass.

I love you Jackie, I can't just give you everything; otherwise you'd become a spoiled brat, and I would never try and shape you into a rat. I want you to be the best in class but that only happens if you put down the bat, when you stop trying to fight the change I've sown into your heart that's going bad, can't you feel it? You're always so mad, you can feel the presence of the Holy Ghost showing you the right path; yet the flesh doesn't want that to come to pass. 'J' I need you to fight back, I need you to do for me what I did for you way back.

Fight for the only one who truly loves you Jackie, fight for "Dad".

HERE AM I

Here am I, laying down my life, for love, for God, for the 3 in one. There's only one way, the way I want to live, and I want to spend my days shaping the world God intends. There's nothing else worth doing, everything else takes your time and health, the only two things that can multiply your mind and heart's wealth; so why waste? Why rot in a lie till the day you die? From level 1 to level 99 is why we're alive.

What do you gain from letting fear run your game? A life where you constantly shake from "the past might come again one day"; only reinsulates a poison robbing you of choices that could set you free if you'd make the voyage. A stone wrapped around your bones where if you cut the rope you'd finally be buoyant. The blade has always been in your hands, just look around, many who've more pain than you have already gotten their life back in their hands.

Look, you may hate me, I used to hate it to, being exposed to absolute truths. But the only way to feel better in a world where we suffer is to understand the reason behind its nature. "Forever happy" isn't heaven, it's a prison; religion masquerades as "the reason" for why you have "listen!!!", the reason you're alive is to experience life; and life is so much more alive when you find out why the light is better than the other side.

But to appreciate God, you have to know what the devil feels like.

HORSE AMONG "HORSES"

Since young, there was always one horse among the herd who loved to run, as the others got older they got colder to their nature "why run day and night when we can lie down and enjoy life", the 'one' didn't understand this "we're made to push our limits, what happened to 'being the fastest'?". They scoffed "bug off, we're made to eat grass that's soft, not run till our hooves fall off", the one looked at the many sadly "fine, enjoy your 'life' fully".

The many continued like this for years, getting big and plump they had no fears "SEE!!! Nothing to worry, only better days are coming here!!!" they would gloat, yet the one still showed no sign of repose, he would dash 'to and fro' for what could he lose? He showed he stood for what the others would not, never leaving the mentality of his original thought, he knew "one day I'll be the fastest of them all".

Then one day while the herd was munching away; suddenly they heard the scream of little "Daisy May", she was being chased by the mountain lion "Moravay". The mom and dad gave all they had but their ankles snapped from being to fat, the cat laughed as he closed in on the young foal from the back, and as he attacked; the once young 'one' was now a stallion that rammed the devilish cat.

"YOU THINK YOU'RE FAST!?!" yelled the cat, "THE FASTEST THERE IS!!!" The stallion snapped back, Moravay pounced for the throat but was met with a twist rear kick to the nose. And as the devil was laid out cold; the others finally realized the importance of fulfilling one's role.

THE "HERO" AND THE "COWARD"

There was a hero who was known throughout the land for slaying dragons, after each slay there was a bar where he would spend his change, a beggar was always there looking more somber every time he came through the door. So he had to ask "why are you always so sad? Cheer up, here, have a few on me, life ain't that bad". The beggar laughed "thank you friend, thanks for wasting your pennies on someone who's even less".

The knight sat down "I'll pay your debt here if you tell me an inkling of why you're so down". The beggar gave a suspicious side eye "fine... I was once a warrior of great might, but when it came time to lay down my life I shied away like a cowardly fly", "that's it? That's all the you're going to give me?" the knight bitterly vied. "You said an inkling, not the whole thing, now pay what you promised me", the knight became very displeased "here's the money you piece of meat".

He stormed out in a fit of rage, and right as he was about to curse the place a dragon began storming the palace's gates. He ran toward the winged-terror and as he got closer he noticed this was no ordinary horror but an ancient dragon of thunder, never before has lightning been a weapon he prepared for, just ice and fire, but he was determined "today, I slay a god of thunder" his mind fawning over the glory that would come after.

He roared out "COWARD!!! FACE ME ON THE BATTLEGROUND!!!" for he knew a dragon's pride was the easiest way to bring them down. Suddenly in a flash of light the beast had crashed right in front of stunned knight, blinded by the light; all he heard after was a voice that made his heart tremble "What did you say to me mortal?". Regaining his sight he realized this monster was 10x the size of the normal dragons he'd usually fight. As tall as the gates of hades, shaking, he got ready "you'll fall like the rest, you MONSTROSITY!!!"

Without warning; lightning hit the metal shield he clung to for security, and with metal plating covering his body he was instantly convulsing in an agony beyond describing. The pain only stopped for a moment. Just long enough to hear the dragon gasping from how hard he was laughing, he began crying "please forgive me, I knew not how mighty you actually were, great titan", "begging won't save you now, keep on pretending to be proud, at least that way you won't die like a clown."

Then the great horror prepared another round of thunder, and as the knight was completely defeated from the first blow he suffered; he couldn't find any will to muster, he merely thought "this is it, I'll die a coward". But just before the final blow could be delivered an arrow pierced the eye of the monster. The creature screamed "WHO DARES ATTACK ME!!!", the knight's eyes raised to find it was the beggar who was sad all the time. "You know who!!! You snake-bellied fool!!!"

"Beowulf? We had an agreement!!! I stay alive and you have eternal life, have you forgotten you'll die?" the titan cried. "I haven't forgotten, I can no longer stand by and let my soul go rotten from knowing I've allowed you to kill thousands for my own insignificant life"."YOU'RE DEAD BEOWULF!!!" roared the dragon, as he mustered another round of lightning; suddenly he fell to the ground lifeless. Beowulf smiled "looks like he wasn't immune to the strongest poison".

He looked to the knight and said "Never just fight for your own life, fight for little lights that make this world so bright, for if even one is extinguished then darkness will certainly overshadow the light, now get up. Continue the fight" with that he fell down. Silently weeping; he whispered to himself "God, please forgive me, the heart I have is human, not of an angel, please forgive the sins of a devil".

THE DEAD MAN

Inside the mind of the dead man

"Everything about life is a horror, best to get pleasure whenever, the only friends that have ever done me any favors are my favorite brands of liquor. My girl only loves me for what I offer; so if she ever steps out of line I'll drop her faster than a bag of rice. Life is hard enough without having to deal with all her stuff, why can't she just shut up when she sees the boiling of my blood? My 'family' is no better, always passively begging for some kind of 'hand over'.

One day I'll tell them all how I really feel, a couple of drinks should be enough to let the truth spill, then maybe they'll think twice before seeking to make me ill. You know what? a combo of pills might help all my rage that's bubbling up release smoother when in flux, that's what I'll do!!! What a great plan, finally unleashing all the pain that's been simmering in my heart's pan, I'll teach them to mess with the 'man', now lets see, where's that bottle?

POP

Here's the first sip coupled with a few little 'friends' *giggle*, this is going to be epic, everyone will finally learn

I'm not to be messed with; just gotta wait a couple more minutes... *time passes* HERE WE GO!!! LETTING IT ALL GO!!!"

dials up mom

"Hey sweetie, everything okay?" Mom calmly cooed. Suddenly, adrenaline pumps mixed with alcohol and drugs sent the poor boy's mind into a deadly fuzz, he became scared and felt deathly drunk "Mum? I'm not okay, I think I'm dying mum", "WHAT!!!" she screamed with chilled blood "BABY!!! HOLD ON!!! I'M CALLING HELP!!! HOLD ON!!!". But little did she know by the time he finished that sentence; he was overdosing on his habits he called his "friends".

Tragic.

BAD RABBIT

There's a tale of a rabbit who chased after every females tail, some rejected, some hesitated, some accepted, but they all agreed he was a strong rabbit. His words were smoother than honey, his body was something of stories, and his eyes captivated you unwittingly. Clever he was, by the time a talk was done; many a doe fell in love. Promises of protecting and providing for the kids, a buck females dream to be with.

Yet, after the play he'd run away, getting mad over the smallest things he'd eventually say "it's not you, it's me okay, it's best if I just stay away", a trickster, the colony gave him a disgraceful name "the bad rabbit and his games". Over time every doe in the warren married good bucks to take care of them, but because of how the "bad rabbit" damaged them; it made it hard on the males to undo all the insecurity the bad one inflicted.

One day they all banded together and made a decision "he has to die for what he's done to our women", so they devised a plan of great deception to lure him into the open. All the bucks for the past few days were going into the farmers garden and destroying everything; so he'd be determined to "KILL THE VARMINTS!!!" by the time they convinced bad rabbit "one of our young daughters has wandered away".

Of course he went looking, of course he assumed she went looking for food for the colony, and of course when he entered the garden there the farmer was… Scoped in, waiting for the "Bad Rabbit" with blood boiling.

LORD HEAL ME

I know it's wrong, this addiction, I can't remember how long I've been afflicted. Its taken root in my heart, it's to deep to reach with just my arm, please lord; remove the leeches in the dark. Take away the desires of this decaying corpse; and create in me one of your wonderful works, you're the only one who can take the dirt; and cleanse away all this hardened earth. It calls to me, they want my soul, save me lord, from my sins of old.

I can't do this alone, I've tried it before, to revive these bones, will take a miracle from the lord. These scars stain my mind, my body is always trying to hide, lord it hurts, please bring me life. My soul is weighed down by rocks, each; etched with a spike of shame, I can't breathe God; save me from this pain, I'm beginning to hate the sound of my own name. I have faith you'll won't condemn the building you're working to recreate.

I'm a dog with the plague, please keep holding me through madness that escapes. I'm trying to be someone different while my reflection screams "THERE IS NO DIFFERENCE!!!", a war is waged inside the mind of a boy who's never been loved the right way, I want to believe, it's my nerves that roar to stay away. Every time I began to build better days; the devil within steals it away. My own actions, my own habits, always, destroy what I create.

That why I need you, because without you, I'm just a man whose reflection he hates.

THE EMPTY MAN

I see him from time to time, a man with an emptiness that stretches through time, I've seen the water-scars beneath his eyes, it makes me cry; for what he must feel inside... I shudder for the ghosts that haunt his mind. The depth of his thought for why he may never find 'the one' at all; is enough to make a heart of stone go soft, holding the faintest hope his love might be at the top of his wall; he slams his fingers into the rock, with bloody hands, he claws.

No smile, no frown, just a numbness that pushes him to find his angel in the clouds. He craves for nothing else, just a heart; he can share his wealth. How far has he travelled through hell? His feet are beaten to the bone, how has he done this; all alone? He doesn't bleed, that would mean to have heart that beats, his eyes hold only the frost of ice, a dead stare, fixed on a horizon whispering in the air "she's out here somewhere".

I wish I could help him, to tell him anything that might quell the pain inside him, but he won't listen, deaf from all the lies that previously bewitched him; he only hears and sees the answer he believes he needs. And what an answer it is, who could blame him? Walking in an underworld where you're treated as faceless; who can blame him for wanting to hear his name cooed from a lover's lips with purpose? To hear a tone of confidence that says "I'll love you even in weakness" I know that would heal his sickness.

And I hope he finds it.

THE WEIGHT

The privileged will never understand, already granted the finer things in life; they naturally identify with "special rights", crystalizing a truth that's behind everyones eyes; they effortlessly climb, for no one ever tried to dim their light. A great mother, father, brothers and sisters, the odds of growing into a great soul is ever in their favor. But for the others trapped in squalor for the sins of their fathers; that seems like a fairytale reserved only for the "favored".

Surrounded by lies disguised as truth; what could a child possibly do? "YOU'RE A MISTAKE!!!", "YOU CANT DO ANYTHING!!!", "THE ONLY THING YOU'RE GOOD FOR IS COOKING AND CLEANING!!!". Even if they get away, the wrathful voices remain, the lashes they would take only further engraved the same mind passed down from cowards who blame rather than refining their name.

It's sad, it makes me mad, for when they stumble or fall; now they feel the weight of the words to be evermore strong. Many have grown, many are painfully alone, and for the lies of old; they begin to wonder about the rope. "I'll never change, I know I have to or die sickly and depraved; but how can I when I keep craving the 'old days'? Maybe I am a mistake, maybe the only thing I'm good for is the grave, I should just give up and accept I'll always be this way".

And those words will continue to crush, continue turning their spirit to mush, all for a world that hates itself just as much; for not shedding the husk stopping them from flying off into the dusk. Even if you relapse from fear; don't ever think you're the same old mirror. You feel guilt, as you should, you want to be better, and better requires feeling the fire from the burning of your old wood. Let it inspire you, let the mere action be the proof, you're no longer the old fool

But a royal in training learning how to rule.

THE EAGLES

What an inspiration, eagles soar with a mighty roar, they must symbolize what it takes to be a free spirit in the world. Eyes shaper than a lion's; they see opportunity without even trying, and how quick, even the most elusive can barely give them the slip, gos to show your wit must be able to crack like a whip if you're going to try and live outside the norm of societal whims. Able to drop on golden moments without being afraid of the diving fall.

Taking the lead with fierce speed is needed to earn the right to live free, rabbits have holes in the ground, hounds have the master's house, but eagles fly high above the mounds; for it's in their nature to perch proud while waiting for their next meal to just make a sound, don't you see? You have to know you'll never stay down, you have to accept it's just in your nature to strengthen your wings to fly around.

Let the other's envy and mock, for while they talk; you'll keep your mentality locked, throwing the trash of your past no longer affects you as bad; because now you understand no one but you can prove how "that was just a broken me from way back", let them laugh, let them continue their fruitless plans to try and put the chains of shame back upon your back, the past can't help you win, but it can show you the consequences from how you used to live.

And let's be honest, you can't fly if you're drinking poison.

MOTHER?

Mom? I hope you're still alive, I regret the things I said, you did what you could with the demons inside your head. I was young, angry, boiling blood. When deep inside was the very same anger that's plagued our family's blood. You held me, you fed me, you gave me a life filled with joy and understanding. I feel like such a bastard, such a cancer, for the words I used to slander your character, I know you've already forgiven me, but please understand; my actions will haunt me, I can't call myself a man.

You gave so much, worked so hard I never got to see you to much, you will probably be my first and final *true* love. I was always a momma's boy, your hugs brought so much warmth when my heart felt destroyed, and now I don't even know if you're alive, I wish I didn't waste so much time, I'm wresting with the curses of our bloodline; but I know I could do better, please hold on mother. Hold on for a son who wishes to see you smile forever.

I have so many presents and gifts I can barely wait to give; from a life I'm still cultivating within. I'm at war with my own madness; but I'll be DAMNED before I let these demons take us, I'll slash and cut, smash and crush, destroy anything seeking to bring destruction upon the only family I've ever loved. You taught me how to love, gave me a heart as bright as the golden sun, I owe you so much, please mom… Hold on for your coming son.

EPILOGUE

**A New Book
Is
Coming Soon!!!
;-)
2025**

Support the author!
**REVIEW THE BOOK ON AMAZON!
:]
(Or other platforms too)**
THANK YOU FAMILY <3

Acknowledgments

I would like to thank myself.
I want to thank myself for not giving up.
Thank you Jack for not losing your mind.
Thank you for choosing to live in a world that tried to crush your heart.
Thank you for continuing to write despite all the pain you were going through.
Thank you for still having a child like wonder and love for creation.
Thank you for choosing God and not the flesh.
Thank you for loving me enough to change for me.
But most of all I want to thank Jesus Christ for pulling me out from the water from which I was drowning, thank you Lord.

Amen

www.ingramcontent.com/pod-product-compliance
Lightning Source LLC
LaVergne TN
LVHW041247080426
835510LV00009B/627